How To...
Play Blues Fusion Guitar

By Joe Charupakorn

To access audio visit:
www.halleonard.com/mylibrary

Enter Code
7758-0216-3583-6131

ISBN 978-1-4950-0097-3

HAL•LEONARD®
CORPORATION

7777 W. BLUEMOUND RD. P.O. BOX 13819 MILWAUKEE, WI 53213

In Australia Contact:
Hal Leonard Australia Pty. Ltd.
4 Lentara Court
Cheltenham, Victoria, 3192 Australia
Email: ausadmin@halleonard.com.au

Visit Hal Leonard Online at
www.halleonard.com

CONTENTS

INTRODUCTION

Blues fusion merges the soulfulness of the blues with the sophistication of jazz. In *How to Play Blues Fusion Guitar*, we'll study the key elements of this style—what scales, chords, and arpeggios are most commonly used, and how to use them. We'll also take a look at some examples in the style of artists like Robben Ford, Larry Carlton, Eric Johnson, Joe Bonamassa, Matt Schofield, Mike Stern, Scott Henderson, and John Scofield, to see how these masters put their own unique spin on the blues fusion format.

AUDIO

Music examples accompany the lessons, so you can hear what the material being taught sounds like. Backing tracks are also provided so you can jam along. To access all of the audio examples that accompany this book, simply go to **www.halleonard.com/mylibrary** and enter the code found on page 1. The examples that include audio are marked with an icon throughout the book.

Joe Charupakorn: guitars

Chad Johnson: additional rhythm guitars, bass, keyboards, and drums

ABOUT THE AUTHOR

New York City native Joe Charupakorn is a guitarist, editor, and best-selling author. He has written numerous instructional books for Hal Leonard Corporation. His books are available worldwide and have been translated into many languages. Visit him on the web at **joecharupakorn.com**.

HOW TO USE THIS BOOK

For each lesson chapter, try playing along with the music examples. When you've gotten them under your fingers, create your own phrases and use the backing tracks to practice over. This is an important step because you need to be able to play your licks in a real context—i.e., against a real groove and in time. The last step is to try and use the material in a live performing situation. This can be the trickiest part, and it will probably take some time to really get the lines to sound organic. But the results are well worth the effort.

After you've comfortably mastered a phrase or concept, try transposing it to different keys. Also, map out different fingerings (on different strings, etc.) so you won't be limited to knowing only one way to play something. Ultimately, the goal is to be able to play anything that you hear in your head.

GEAR

Gear is one part of the equation that can't be overlooked. While nothing can equal sheer playing ability, having the right tone is an integral part of copping the blues fusion vibe. One way to put together a rig is to base it on what your favorite artists use. For reference, we'll look at some of the equipment used by the masters. Note that players tend to change gear from time to time, but these lists should give you a ballpark estimate as to what is needed for a certain sound.

Blues fusion artists are notoriously fastidious when it comes to equipment and tone. Some of the gear used by the greats can be exorbitantly priced or even currently unavailable for purchase, so at the end of this chapter, we'll also look at alternate choices that can get you similar results.

Zendrive pedal

Dumble amp

335-type guitar

SETUPS OF THE STARS

Robben Ford

- **Guitars:** 1966 Epiphone Riviera, Taku Sakashta custom guitar, 1960 Fender Telecaster, 1957 Gibson goldtop Les Paul

- **Amps:** Dumble Overdrive Special, Dumble 2x12 cab equipped with Celestion G12-65 8 ohm speakers, Fender Super Reverbs, Fender tweed Deluxe

- **Effects:** TC Electronic 2290 digital delay (rackmount), Vox wah, Ernie Ball volume pedal, Hermida Audio Zendrive, TC Electronic PolyTune Mini, Vertex-modded Boss FV-500 volume pedal with expression control, Vertex Boost, Strymon TimeLine digital delay, Roland EV-5 expression pedal, TC Electronic Hall of Fame reverb, Voodoo Lab Pedal Power

- **Strings and Picks:** D'Addario .010–.046 strings, Planet Waves heavy picks

Larry Carlton

- **Guitars:** Gibson Larry Carlton signature ES-335, 1969 Gibson ES-335, 1968 Gibson ES-335, 1955 Gibson Les Paul Special TV, 1954 Fender Telecaster, 1962 Fender Stratocaster, Valley Arts T-style, Valley Arts acoustic

- **Amps:** Bludotone Bludo-Drive 100/50, Bludotone 1x12 cab with an Electro-Voice EVM12L speaker, Bludotone 50/25 (studio), Fender tweed Deluxe

- **Effects:** Korg Pitchblack tuner, Sho-Bud volume pedal, Dunlop Cry Baby wah, Tanabe Zenkudo overdrive, Visual Sound Liquid Chorus, TC Electronic Hall of Fame reverb, Providence DLY-4 Chrono digital delay, Roland SDE-1000 digital delay (rackmount), TC Electronic 1210 stereo chorus flanger (rackmount), Lexicon MX400 multi-effects (rackmount)

- **Strings and Picks:** D'Adarrio .010–.052 strings (electric), D'Adarrio .011–.052 strings (acoustic)

Eric Johnson

- **Guitars:** 1957 Fender Stratocaster (with Seymour Duncan antiquity pickups in the bridge and middle positions), Fender Eric Johnson signature Stratocaster, 1964 Gibson SG, Martin MC-40 signature acoustic

- **Amps:** Marshall 100W head, 1968 Marshall 50W head, Fender Twin Reverb, Dumble, Fulton-Webb head, 1960s Marshall 4x12 cab equipped with Celestions

- **Effects:** BK Butler Tube Driver, Ibanez TS808 Vintage Tube Screamer reissue, Dunlop Eric Johnson signature Fuzz Face, TC Electronic SCF (stereo chorus flanger), Electro-Harmonix Memory Man delay, Boss DD-2 digital delay, MXR 1500 digital delay (rackmount), Echoplex tape delay, Toadworks Barracuda flanger

- **Strings and Picks:** GHS .010–.050 strings, Dunlop Eric Johnson signature Jazz III picks

Joe Bonamassa

- **Guitars:** Gibson Joe Bonamassa signature ES-335, Gibson Joe Bonamassa signature Les Paul, 1959 Gibson Les Paul, 1963 non-tremolo Gibson Firebird 1, tremolo-equipped 1966 polaris white Gibson Firebird 1, Ernie Ball/Music Man Dark Morse, Ernie Ball/Music Man John Petrucci BFR baritone

- **Amps:** Dumble Overdrive Special, Carol Ann JB-100 Joe Bonamassa signature model, Van Weelden Twinkleland (Bonamassa runs a multi-amp setup that includes the above-mentioned amps plus Marshall Silver Jubilee 100W heads)

- **Effects:** Klon Centaur overdrive, Ibanez TS808 Vintage Tube Screamer reissue, MXR FET Driver, Way Huge Pork Loin overdrive, Dunlop Bonamassa Fuzz Face, Dunlop Joe Bonamassa Cry Baby wah, Fulltone Supra-Trem, Electro-Harmonix Micro POG (polyphonic octave generator), Boss DD-3 digital delay, MXR Micro Flanger, Hughes & Kettner Rotosphere rotary speaker simulator, Boss RV-5 reverb, Voodoo Labs Pedal Power 2, Dumbleator effects loop, TC Electronic 2290 digital delay (rackmount)

- **Strings and Picks:** Ernie Ball Cobalt Slinky .011–.052 strings, gold Dunlop Jazz III picks

Matt Schofield

- **Guitars:** SVL 61 Daytona, SVL 59, SVL 60, 1961 Fender Stratocaster

- **Amps:** Two-Rock Matt Schofield signature 50W head, Two-Rock 4x10 cab with Eminence Ragin Cajun speakers or a Bludotone ported 1x12 cabinet with an EVM12L speaker, 1964 Fender Super Reverb with four Celestion G10 Gold speakers

- **Effects:** Free the Tone Matt Schofield Signature SOV-2 overdrive, Vemuram Jan Ray overdrive, Mad Professor Deep Blue digital delay, Vertex Axis wah, Providence DLY-4 Chrono digital delay, Fulltone Tube Tape Echo, Fuchs Verbrator reverb/effects loop

- **Strings and Picks:** Curt Mangan Matt Schofield signature .011–.054 strings, Curt Mangan 1.0mm Curtex picks

Mike Stern

- **Guitars:** Yamaha Mike Stern signature Pacifica 1511MS

- **Amps:** Pearce G1 head, Hartke 4x10 cab with JBL speakers, Yamaha G-100 212 II combo with two Electro-Voice 12" speakers, Fender '65 Twin Reverb reissue

- **Effects:** Boss DS-1 distortion, Keeley-modded Boss SD-1 Super Overdrive, Boss DD-3 digital delay, Boss OC-2 octave, Boss PSM-5 power supply, DigiTech Multi-Chorus, Yamaha SPX-90 multi-effects (rackmount)

- **Strings and Picks:** Fender .010–.038 strings (with an .011 on top), Fender medium picks

John Scofield

- **Guitars:** Ibanez John Scofield signature AS200, Fender Custom Shop Stratocaster, Ibanez T-style

- **Amps:** Vox AC30TB

- **Effects:** ProCo Rat overdrive, J. Rockett Blue Note overdrive, TC Electronic PolyTune Mini, Vertex Axis Wah, Vertex-modded Boss GE-7 graphic equalizer, Vertex-modded Boss CE-3 chorus, Neunaber Audio Effects USA Wet Reverb, Boomerang Phrase Sampler, Electro-Harmonix Micro Synth, DigiTech Whammy XP100

- **Strings and Picks:** D'Adarrio .011–.049 strings, Dunlop Delrin 2mm picks

Scott Henderson

- **Guitars:** Suhr Scott Henderson signature

- **Amps:** Suhr SH-100, Kerry Wright 4x12 open-back cabinet with 8 ohm Celestion Greenback speakers, Dumble modded Fender Bandmaster

- **Effects:** Xotic Effects RC Booster, Maxon SD-9 distortion, Fulltone Octafuzz, Zvex Fuzz Factory, modded Arion SCH-1 chorus, Vertex Axis Wah, E.W.S. Subtle Volume Control, Boss SE-70 multi-effects (rackmount), Tech 21 Midi Mouse, Boss RC-2 noise suppressor, Snark SN-8 tuner

- **Strings and Picks:** D'Adarrio .010–.046 strings, Fender heavy picks

CREATING YOUR OWN RIG

Guitars

If you're a blues fusion aficionado, you'll likely gravitate toward one of four types of guitars: the Stratocaster, Telecaster, Les Paul, or ES-335. Fender and Gibson are the two biggest brands on the market, but some other makers worth checking out are Suhr, Tom Anderson, K-Line, Lentz, D'Pergo, Ron Kirn, Creston, Collings, and Artinger, among many others.

If you don't already have a guitar and are not sure what to get, look through the lists and narrow things down by choosing a type based on a player you like. For example, Larry Carlton is nicknamed "Mr. 335." If you're a Carlton fan, an ES-335-type would definitely be a good choice. On the other hand, if you prefer the distinctly Strat sounds that someone like Matt Schofield gets, then a Strat is probably the right instrument for you. You don't necessarily have to get the exact model that your favorite artist uses, but something similar will get you close to the sound that you are after.

Amps

Amps are the next part of the equation and can play a tremendous role in shaping your sound. Among blues fusion luminaries like Robben Ford, Larry Carlton, and Joe Bonamassa, the amp of choice is the Overdrive Special made by Alexander "Howard" Dumble. Eric Johnson has also used Dumbles throughout his career, and Scott Henderson has used a Fender Bandmaster modified by Dumble. But don't plan on just going to the local guitar store and picking up a Dumble in your spare time. These extremely rare amps are made in very limited numbers on special order for only select clients and are perhaps the most expensive amps in history, with prices hitting the mid five figures and climbing!

If a Dumble is out of reach (as is the case with most mortals), there are many great alternatives ("Dumble clones") on the market today. Many of today's biggest names in blues fusion are using Dumble-inspired amps in their rigs. Even Joe Bonamassa, who owns a real Dumble, has several Dumble-flavored amps in his arsenal. Two-Rock, Glaswerks, and Bludotone are some of the best makers of Dumble-style amps on the market today.

On the other hand, you might not necessarily need or want a boutique amp. Mike Stern uses an old solid-state Yamaha G-100 212 II combo and gets a signature sound with it. Pat Metheny and Robben Ford also used the Yamaha G100 at one point, back in the day. When he's on the road, Scott Henderson rents Fender Hot Rod Deluxes and Marshall DSL 401s: two very common and easy-to-find amps.

Effects

Of all the effects out there, the most popular is the overdrive/distortion pedal. Even if your amp isn't a high-end boutique model, a great dirt pedal can help you get killer tones.

We looked at some options for getting the Dumble sound—so desired by many blues fusion players—through "Dumble clone" amps. Another alternative, and also an economical way to get close to the Dumble sound, is via one of the many Dumble-flavored pedals on the market nowadays. One pedal especially worthy of note is the Hermida Audio Zendrive (now manufactured by Lovepedal), which was designed by Alfonso Hermida with Robben Ford's tone in mind. When Ford tried the Zendrive, he loved it so much that he used it on tour, plugging it into rented Fender Twin Reverbs or Super Reverbs. Other Dumble-inspired pedals include the Custom Tones Ethos, Tanabe Zenkudo (which Larry Carlton uses), and the Mad Professor Simble.

There are also some pedals that are based on Eric Johnson's tone. The Mad Professor Golden Cello has dirt and delay in one box and does a great rendition of Johnson's "violin" tone. The Hermida Dover Drive was voiced with Johnson's "Righteous" tone in mind and offers great Johnson-esque tones.

If you're not after Dumble or Eric Johnson-type tones, some pedals to consider are the ProCo Rat or the Ibanez Tube Screamer. The ProCo Rat has been a part of John Scofield's signature sound for decades and is a favorite among the more jazz-oriented fusion artists like Bill Frisell, Ben Monder, Kurt Rosenwinkel, and Charles Altura. The Tube Screamer is possibly the most popular (and most copied) overdrive pedal in history, and with good reason; it always delivers. Almost every pro player has or has had a Tube Screamer or some variant of it (many pedals on the market are based on modified Tube Screamer circuits) at some point in their careers.

Between a good guitar, amp, and overdrive/distortion pedal, you'll be able to get a strong fundamental tone. Once you are set with that, it's worth considering adding other types of effects, like delay and reverb, and building from there.

Here's a summary of some great options to consider at several price ranges. Many of these are readily available at most retailers.

- **Guitars:** Fender Stratocaster, Fender Telecaster, Gibson Les Paul, Gibson ES-335, Gibson ES-339, Suhr Classic, Suhr Classic T, Tom Anderson "S" Family Classic, Tom Anderson "T" Family Classic, Collings I-35, Collings SoCo

- **Amps:** Two-Rock Studio Pro, Glaswerks Zingaro, Glaswerks Overdrive Deluxe, Glaswerks Super Overdrive II, Bludotone Ojai, Fender Hot Rod Deluxe

- **Overdrive/Distortion pedals:** Hermida Audio Zendrive, Hermida Audio Dover Drive, Custom Tones Ethos, Tanabe Zenkudo, Mad Professor Simble, Mad Professor Golden Cello, ProCo Rat, Ibanez Tube Screamer, Boss DS-1

- **Delay pedals:** TC Electronic Flashback, Boss DD-3, MXR Carbon Copy, Line 6 DL4, Strymon El Capistan, Strymon TimeLine

- **Reverb pedals:** Boss RV-5, TC Electronic Hall of Fame, Strymon blueSky

It's also worth mentioning that how you play the guitar can have as significant an impact on your tone as the equipment that you use. For example, if you play with your pick-hand fingers, you can get a glassy tone like Robben Ford sometimes gets in his single-note playing. If you play with the rounded edge of a pick, rather than the pointy tip, you'll get a warmer sound with a softer attack. There's a saying that goes, "The tone is in your fingers." The guitar is an expressive instrument with a wide dynamic range. Experiment with getting as many sounds out of it as you can!

The fundamental chords you'll encounter in blues fusion are:

- **maj7** (major seventh chord)

- **m7** (minor seventh chord)

- **7** (dominant seventh chord)

- **m7♭5** (minor seventh flat five chord)

- **6** (major sixth chord)

- **m6** (minor sixth chord)

Later on in this book, you'll learn fancier versions of these chords (with extensions and alterations), but for now, get familiar with these if you don't already know them. Chord fingerings throughout this book are all moveable. To move a shape with open strings, use a barre in place of the open strings.

Major 7

A major seventh chord consists of the root (first note), 3rd, 5th, and 7th degrees of a major scale. You may see this chord referred to as maj7, △, or M7. They all mean the same thing.

For example, Amaj7 is spelled:

A	C♯	E	G♯
1	3	5	7

Here are some common moveable fingerings for this chord:

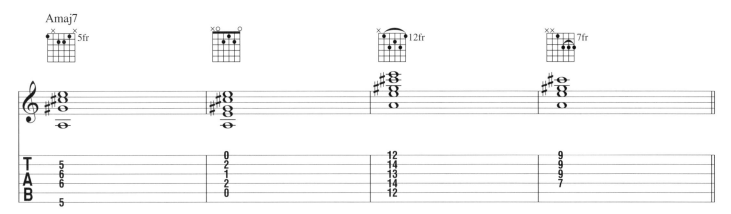

Minor 7

A minor seventh chord consists of the root (first note), ♭3rd, 5th, and ♭7th degrees of a major scale. (Note: There actually are no flatted tones in a major scale; its numeric formula is simply 1–2–3–4–5–6–7. Rather, the indicated tones—3rd and 7th in this case—are flatted to arrive at the chord formula.) You may see this chord referred to as m7, min7, or -7. They all mean the same thing.

Am7 is spelled:

A	C	E	G
1	♭3	5	♭7

Here are some common moveable fingerings:

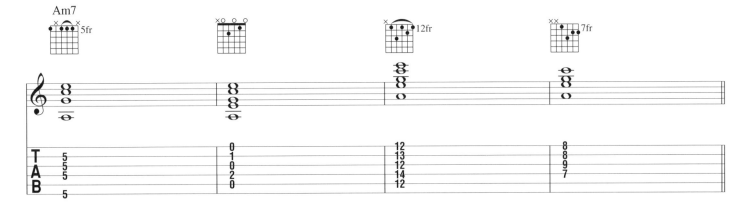

Dominant 7

A dominant seventh chord is usually just referred to by the root followed by the number "7" (for example, A7, D7, E7, etc.). It consists of the root (first note), 3rd, 5th, and ♭7th degrees of a major scale.

A7 is spelled:

A	C♯	E	G
1	3	5	♭7

Here are some common moveable fingerings:

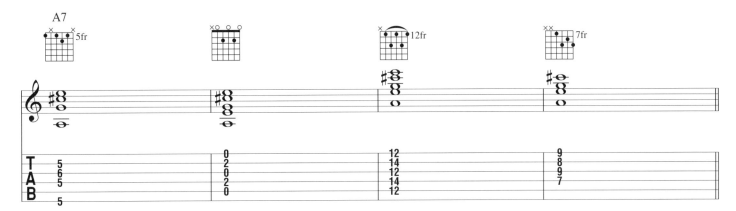

Minor 7♭5

A minor seventh flat 5 chord consists of the root (first note), ♭3rd, ♭5th, and ♭7th degrees of a major scale. You may also see this chord referred to as half diminished or ∅. They both mean the same thing.

Am7♭5 is spelled:

A	C	E♭	G
1	♭3	♭5	♭7

Here are some common moveable fingerings:

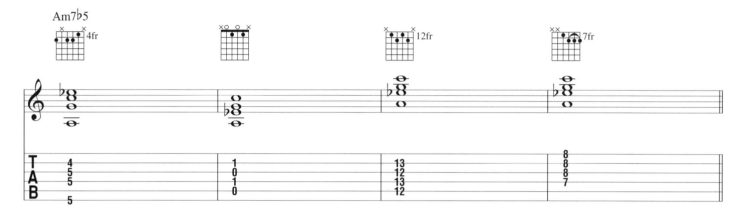

Major 6

A major sixth chord is usually just referred to by the root followed by the number "6" (for example, A6, D6, E6, etc.). It consists of the root (first note), 3rd, 5th, and 6th degrees of a major scale.

A6 is spelled:

A	C♯	E	F♯
1	3	5	6

Here are some common moveable fingerings:

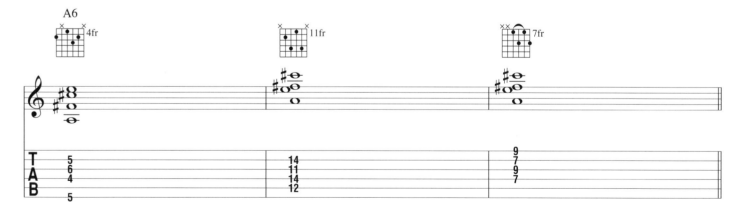

Minor 6

A minor sixth chord consists of the root (first note), ♭3rd, 5th, and 6th degrees of a major scale. You'll see this chord referred to as m6, min6, or -6. They all mean the same thing.

Am6 is spelled:

A	C	E	F♯
1	♭3	5	6

Here are some common moveable fingerings:

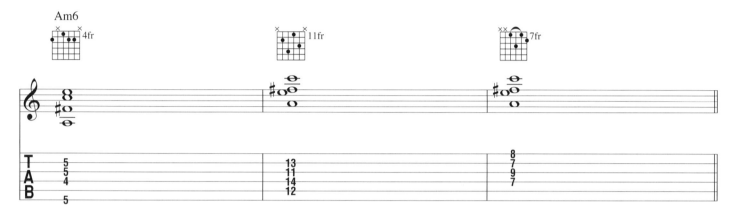

Practice the chords you've just learned with these blues progressions. Play along with these backing tracks and try out different voicings of the same chords.

12-Bar Blues in A

Play-Along 1

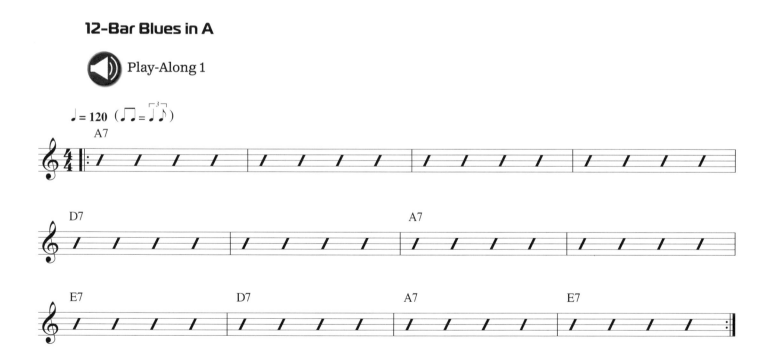

12-Bar Minor Blues in A Minor

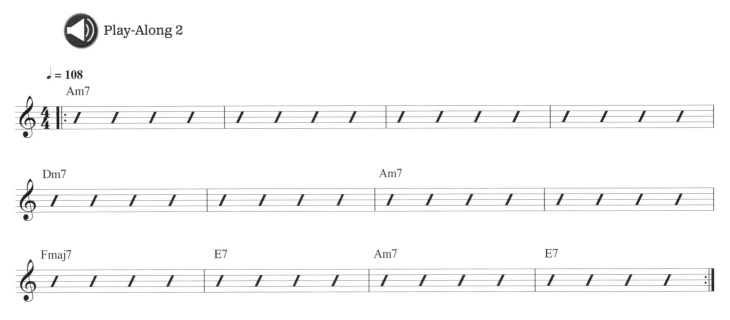

PENTATONIC AND BLUES SCALES

Minor Pentatonic: 1–♭3–4–5–♭7

For blues players, pentatonic scales are where it all begins and ends—many of the greats have forged careers out of using pentatonic scales exclusively! A pentatonic scale is a five-note scale ("penta" means five, and "tonic" means notes). The most common pentatonic scale is the *minor pentatonic scale*, which consists of 1, ♭3, 4, 5, and ♭7. There isn't a single blues player in the world that hasn't played a minor pentatonic scale.

In every major key, three minor pentatonic scales occur diatonically. They are built on the 2nd, 3rd, and 6th degrees of the scale. For example, in the key of A major, there are three minor pentatonic scales: B, C♯, and F♯.

Over major-type chords, the minor pentatonic built on the 6th is often used. For example, in the key of A major, this would be F♯ minor pentatonic.

Over dominant and minor-type chords, the minor pentatonic built on the root is often used. Over minor-type chords, this works well because the minor pentatonic scale contains a ♭3rd.

Dominant-type chords contain a major 3rd, so the minor pentatonic's ♭3rd creates a little bit of a rub. But this clash is actually desirable in blues music and adds a distinctly bluesy quality. Sometimes, when the ♭3 is played over dominant-type chords, blues players like to bend up to the major 3rd. However, they don't always bend it up perfectly in tune everytime. Sometimes they deliberately exploit the tension of sounding the notes "between the cracks."

Technically, if you're playing a ♭3rd over a dominant chord, the note is also the enharmonic equivalent of the ♯9th. This sounds fancy and complicated, but in reality, the ♯9th is a very familiar blues note. It's the note that gave the opening E7♯9 chord of "Purple Haze" its pungency. For a more detailed explanation, check out the Chord Extensions and Alterations chapter on page 55.

Here are five moveable fingerings for A minor pentatonic starting on every scale degree. Memorize these shapes and transpose them to other keys:

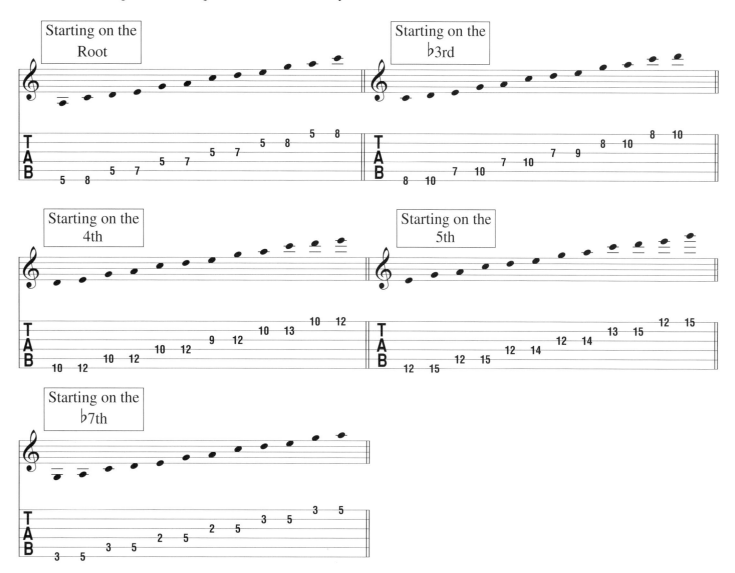

The third-string bend of the 4th to the 5th followed by the unison on the second string and root on the first string in measure 1 of the example below is a classic "must-know" minor pentatonic move. By beat 3 of measure 2, a shift takes us into the second shape of the scale. This little scale fragment on strings 3–1 is sometimes called the Albert King box because many players often imitate his licks (which were actually played much differently due to his unorthodox style) in this position.

Track 1

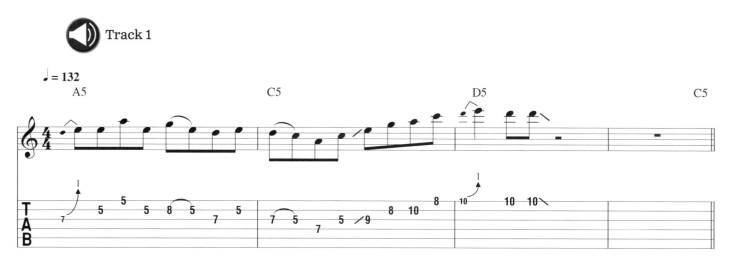

Here's a common variation on the previous lick. The bend followed by two notes is repeated over and over again for a dramatic effect before resolving via a slide to the second-string A note.

Track 2

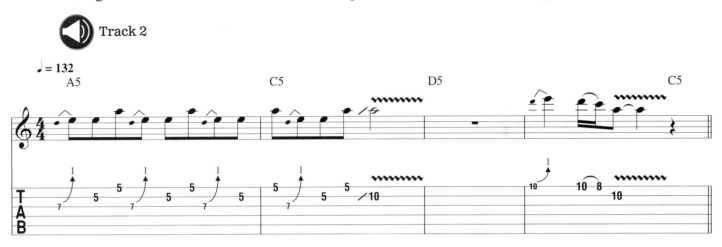

You don't need to play a million different notes to create an effective pentatonic lick. Here, only a few different notes are used, but the triplet rhythm gives the repeated bending motive a dose of energy and forward momentum.

Track 3

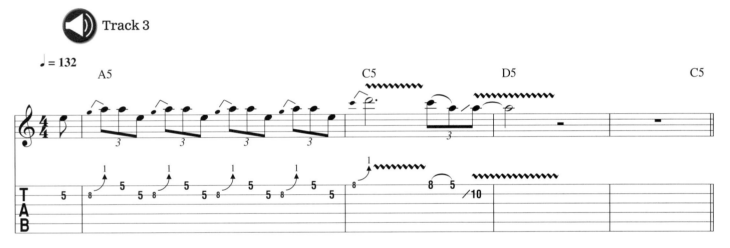

The minor pentatonic scale also lends itself very nicely to riff-based, catchy melodies. Much of the great classic rock riffs were created using pentatonic-based melodies.

Track 4

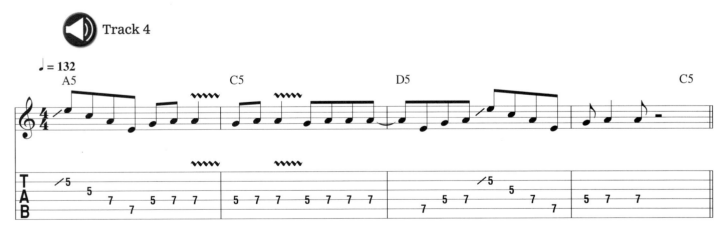

Practice using the A minor pentatonic scale to come up with your own licks against this play-along track.

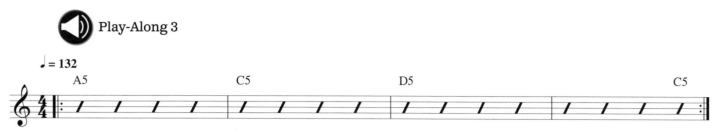

Play-Along 3

♩ = 132

Major Pentatonic: 1–2–3–5–6

The major pentatonic scale is also very common in blues and consists of 1, 2, 3, 5, and 6. In every major key, three major pentatonic scales occur diatonically. They are built on the root, 4th, and 5th degrees. Over major and dominant-type chords, the major pentatonic built on the root is often used.

Here are five moveable fingerings for A major pentatonic starting on every scale degree. As with the minor pentatonic shapes we looked at, memorize these shapes and try transposing them to other keys:

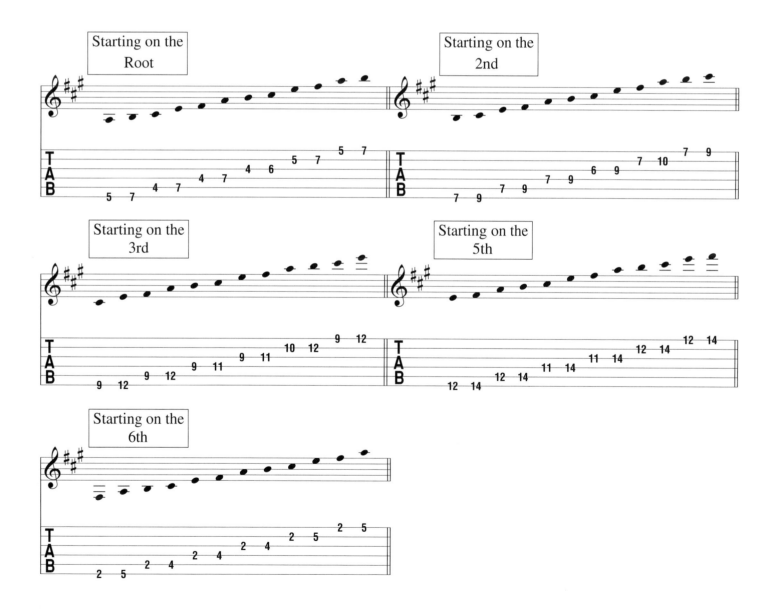

When we looked at minor pentatonic scales, we learned that over major-type chords, the minor pentatonic built on the 6th is often used. Guitarists often refer to this relative minor pentatonic shape for their major pentatonic licks, since it's more familiar and fits under the fingers a little more naturally than the root-position major pentatonic shape. Here, the F# minor pentatonic shape (which shares the same notes as A major pentatonic) is used as the home base.

Track 5

Taking the same idea from the previous example, this lick uses the relative minor fingering to spin out some classic licks. This is a faster version of the bending licks we looked at in the minor pentatonic section.

Track 6

The major pentatonic shape comfortably lends itself to slides and position shifts, as this lick, which traverses three octaves, demonstrates.

Track 7

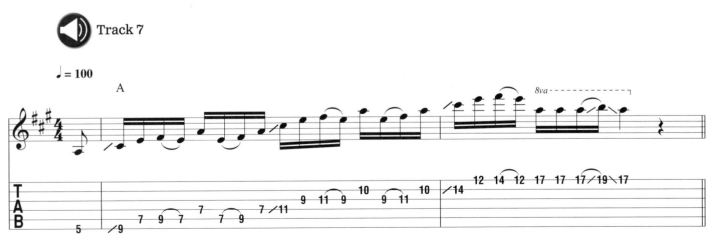

The major pentatonic scale's sweet sound makes it a natural fit for progressions that have a pop or soul vibe.

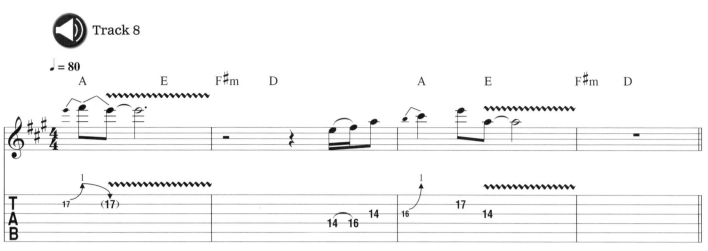

Practice using the A major pentatonic scale to come up with your own licks against these play-along tracks.

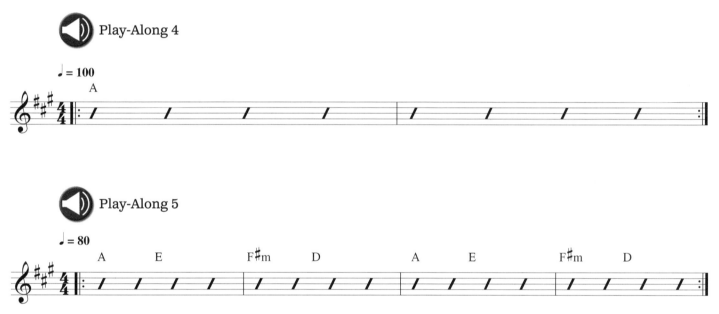

Blues Scale: 1–♭3–4–♭5–5–♭7

Blues scales are minor pentatonic scales with an added ♭5th. As the name implies, they're commonly employed in a bluesy manner. Over dominant and minor-type chords, the blues scale built on the root is often used.

Here are some moveable fingerings for the A blues scale:

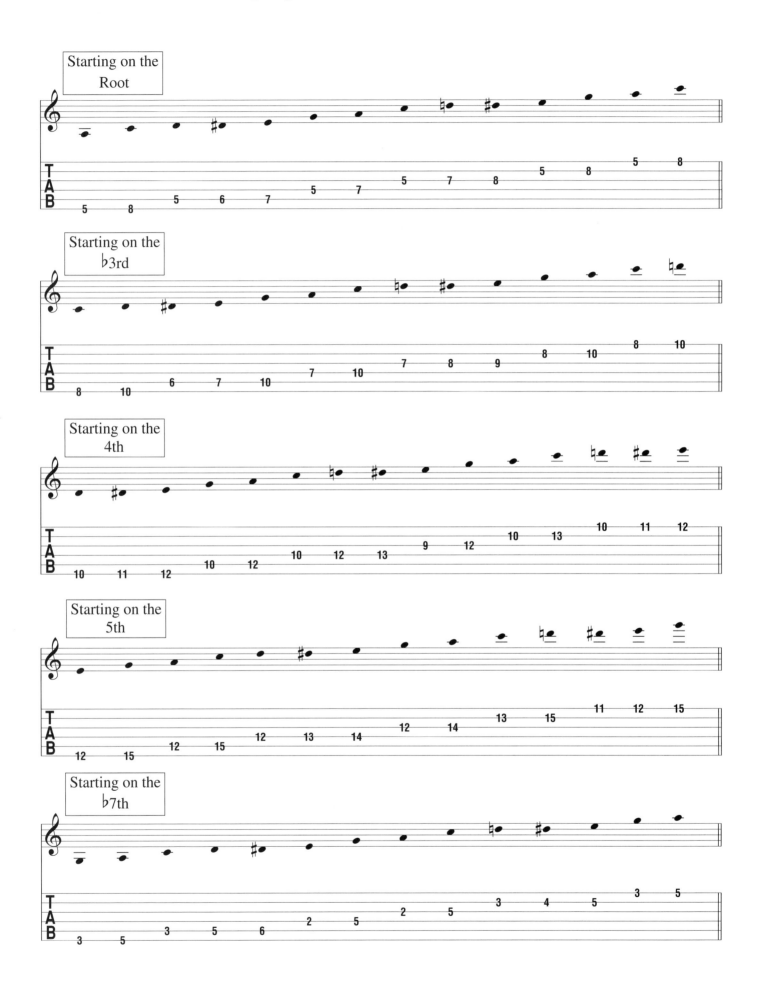

The blues scale's ♭5th is a great way to add spice to your lines. Sometimes players will hold on to the ♭5th for added tension, as demonstrated here in measure 2.

Track 9

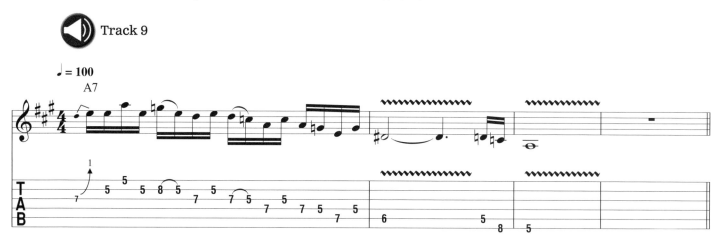

Or you can bend the ♭5th up to the natural 5 for just a smidge of dissonance.

Track 10

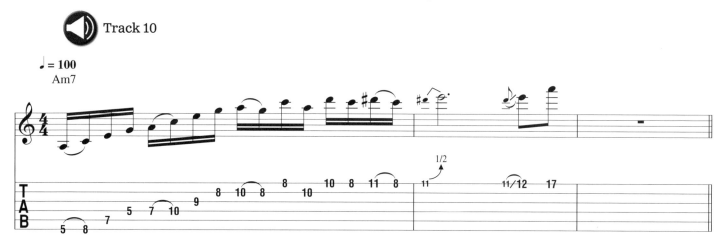

The chromatic notes between the 4th and 5th can lead to some slippery sounds. Check out the rolling chromatics in measure 2, beats 2–3.

Track 11

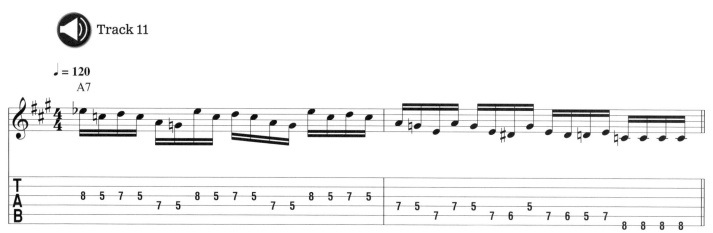

The blues scale's ♭5th can also add an interesting diminished flavor to your lines. A useful idea for this effect is to alternate between the ♭3rd and the ♭5th on the G string and the root and ♭3rd on the high E string, using the sixth-string root-based blues scale fingering. You'll hear this type of effect used by fusion players like Scott Henderson and John Scofield (check out the licks on page 94–95).

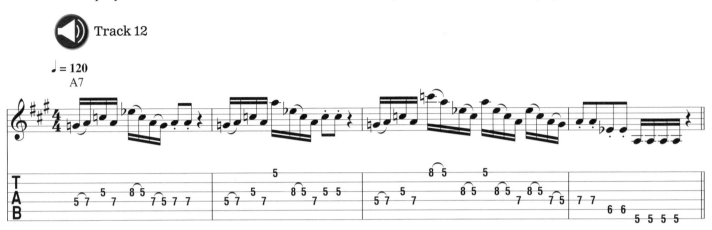

Practice using the A blues scale to come up with your own licks against these play-along tracks.

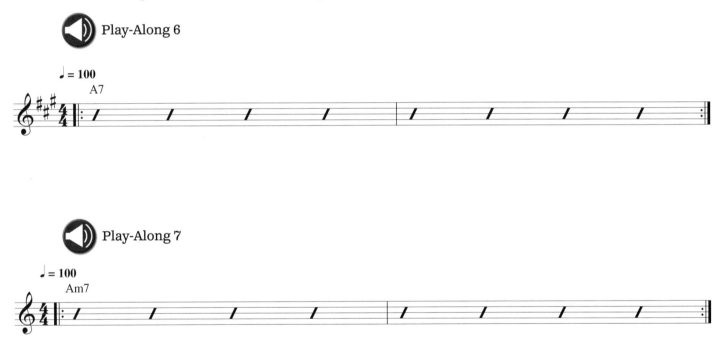

Once you're comfortable with the basic pentatonic and blues scales, you can start experimenting and mixing things up.

Minor 6 Pentatonic: 1–♭3–4–5–6

Blues fusion great Robben Ford often replaces the ♭7th of the minor pentatonic scale with the 6th to create a sweeter sound. This scale can be used over minor or dominant-type chords.

Here are moveable fingerings for the A minor 6 pentatonic scale starting on every scale degree:

This lick starts off with a typical minor pentatonic move, but in measure 2, employs the 6th to get a nice, funky vibe.

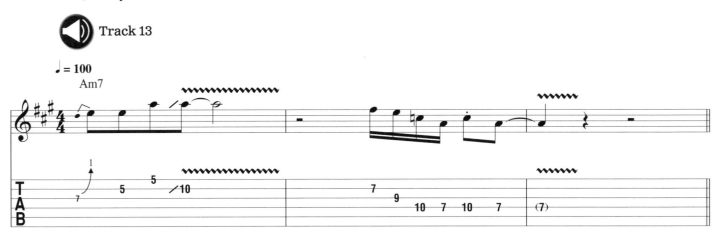

Here's a lick that uses the minor 6 pentatonic scale, played mostly along the high E string, and primarily with dotted quarter notes to create rhythmic tension.

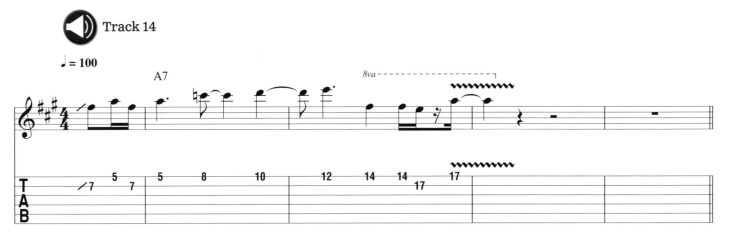

Major/Minor Pentatonic: 1–2–♭3–3–4–5–6–♭7 and
Major/Blues: 1–2–♭3–3–4–♭5–5–6–♭7

The major pentatonic is often combined with the minor pentatonic or the blues scale to form a composite blues scale. One interesting way of looking at it is that the major pentatonic/blues mix results almost in a chromatic scale (with only the ♭2nd, ♭6th, and major 7th missing).

Here's a fingering for the sixth-string root A major/minor pentatonic scale:

And here's a fingering for the sixth-string root A major/blues scale:

This lick is based on an easy-to-visualize hammer-on/pull-off figure from the combined major and minor pentatonic scales.

Track 15

♩ = 100
A7

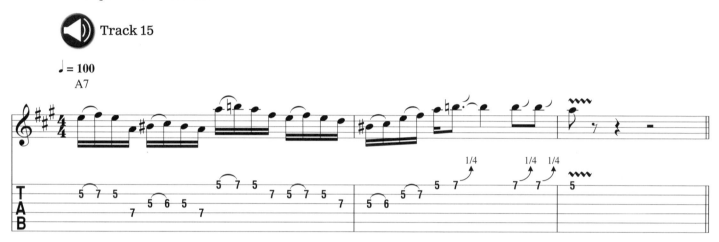

Just because a composite blues scale has a lot of notes doesn't mean you necessarily need to use all of them. Here's a common repeating phrase that gets a lot of mileage out of only a small portion of the scale.

Track 16

♩ = 100
A7

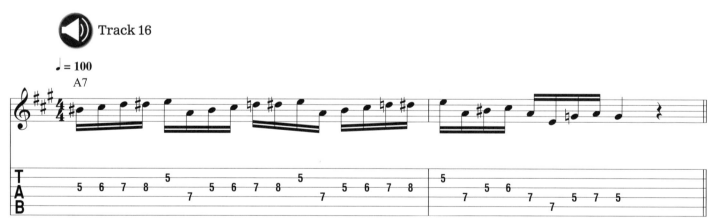

ESSENTIAL SCALES

Blues and fusion collide when players start stepping outside of just purely pentatonic and blues scales and begin integrating others. The most common non-pentatonic or blues scales you'll see are the major (Ionian), Dorian, and Mixolydian scales. There are other modes of the major scale—Lydian, Aeolian, and Locrian—but we'll focus on the three mentioned above because they are seen more often in this genre. Particularly noteworthy are Dorian and Mixolydian, which are the funkiest of the bunch.

Sometimes you'll hear scales referred to as modes and vice versa. For our purposes, both terms essentially mean the same thing.

Major Scale: 1–2–3–4–5–6–7

The *major scale*—also referred to as the Ionian mode—is the foundation for all of Western music. While it's not the first scale that comes to mind when one thinks of blues, the great blues fusion players have found ways to incorporate it into their playing.

To create a major scale, you can use the following *step-pattern* formula:

Whole–Whole–Half–Whole–Whole–Whole–Half

In other words, starting on A, we get:

A–B–C♯– D–E–F♯–G♯–A

A to B = whole step

B to C♯ = whole step

C♯ to D = half step

D to E = whole step

E to F♯ = whole step

F♯ to G♯ = whole step

G♯ to A = half step

For blues playing, one way of thinking about the major scale is that it's like a major pentatonic scale with added 4th and 7th tones.

The most obvious place to use a major scale is over a major seventh-type chord. Here are some moveable fingerings for the A major scale starting on every scale degree:

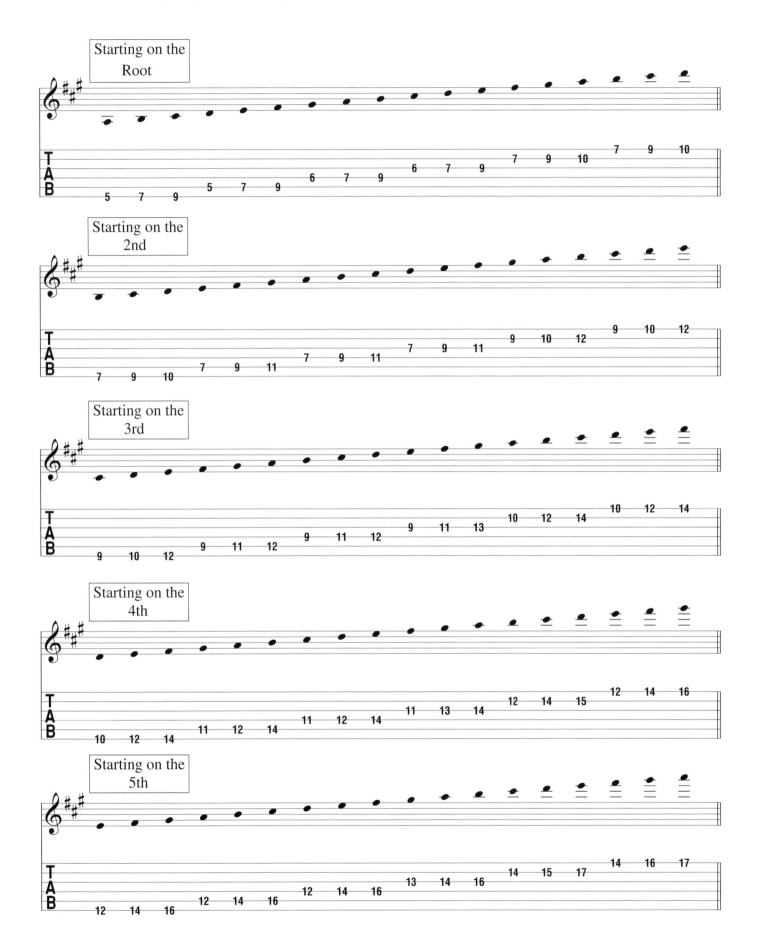

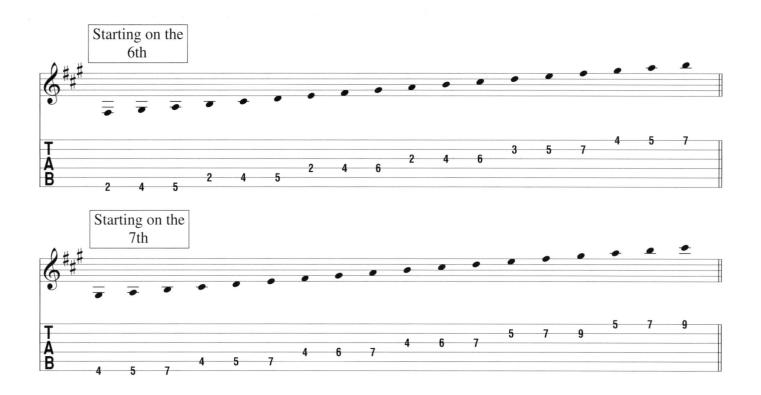

Following are some examples of what the major scale sounds like in a blues fusion context.

The major scale often lends itself to classical-type phrasing where you'll hear long streams of notes. It can be hard to make the major scale sound bluesy, but masters like Larry Carlton have done it very successfully. In this example, blues inflections like slides and bends help add a blues vibe.

Track 17

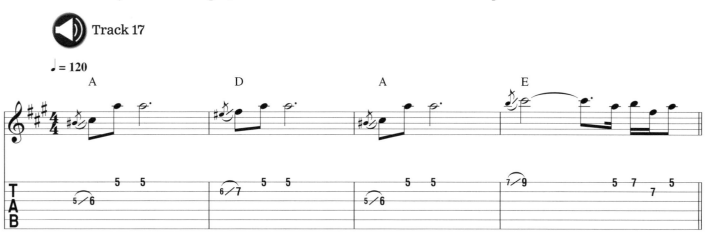

After a quick A triad arpeggio played in triplets, the emphasized G♯ over the D chord in measure 2 adds a nice moment of tension. If this note catches you off guard and sounds unpleasant, your ears may not be used to hearing certain dissonances. You might even think that it sounds wrong. But in phrases like this, that dissonance is actually carefully placed.

Many jazz-oriented players are acutely aware of the impact of every scale note against the underlying chord, choosing their notes appropriately depending on how much tension, color, or release is desired.

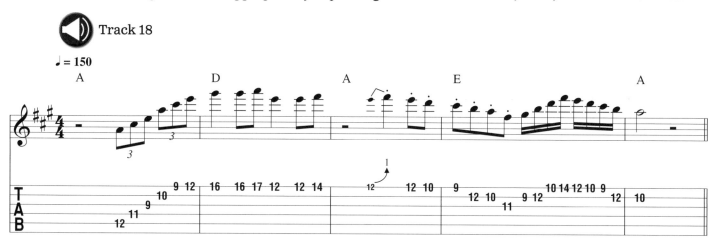

Track 18

♩ = 150

Practice using the A major scale to come up with your own licks against this play-along track.

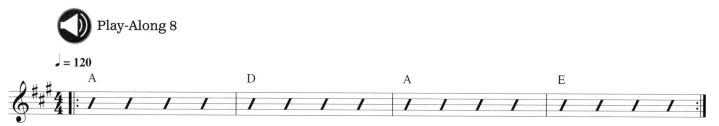

Play-Along 8

♩ = 120

One way to get a major scale line to sound bluesy is to draw primarily from the major pentatonic scale, using the 2nd or 4th sparingly (the presence of these two tones differentiates the major scale from the major pentatonic). Here, A major pentatonic sets the mood for the phrase until measure 4, when G♯ (the 7th) is introduced.

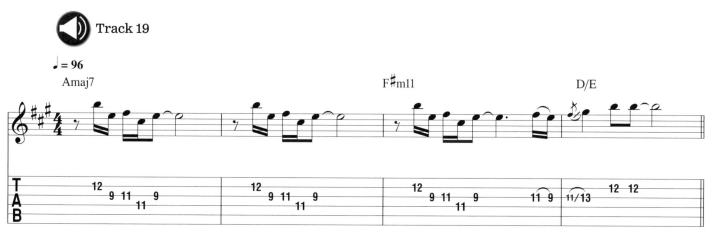

Track 19

♩ = 96

Practice the previous lick against this play-along track. Also practice using the A major scale to come up with your own licks.

Play-Along 9

Again, blurring the line between a major scale and a major pentatonic scale is a good strategy for getting bluesy-sounding major licks. This next example starts off with an A major pentatonic-based motif and then introduces the notes of the complete major scale in measure 3.

Track 20

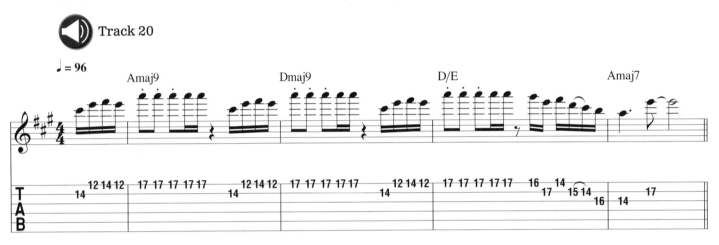

Practice the previous lick against this play-along track. Also practice using the A major scale to come up with your own licks.

Play-Along 10

Dorian: 1–2–♭3–4–5–6–♭7

A very important scale for blues fusion is the *Dorian* scale. Dorian is most commonly used on minor seventh-type chords and can be viewed as a minor pentatonic scale with added 2nd and 6th tones. Back in the day, Carlos Santana popularized this scale in his hit "Oye Como Va," which is a textbook example of the Dorian sound. If you've heard that song, you know what Dorian sounds like.

Here are some moveable fingerings for the A Dorian scale starting on every scale degree:

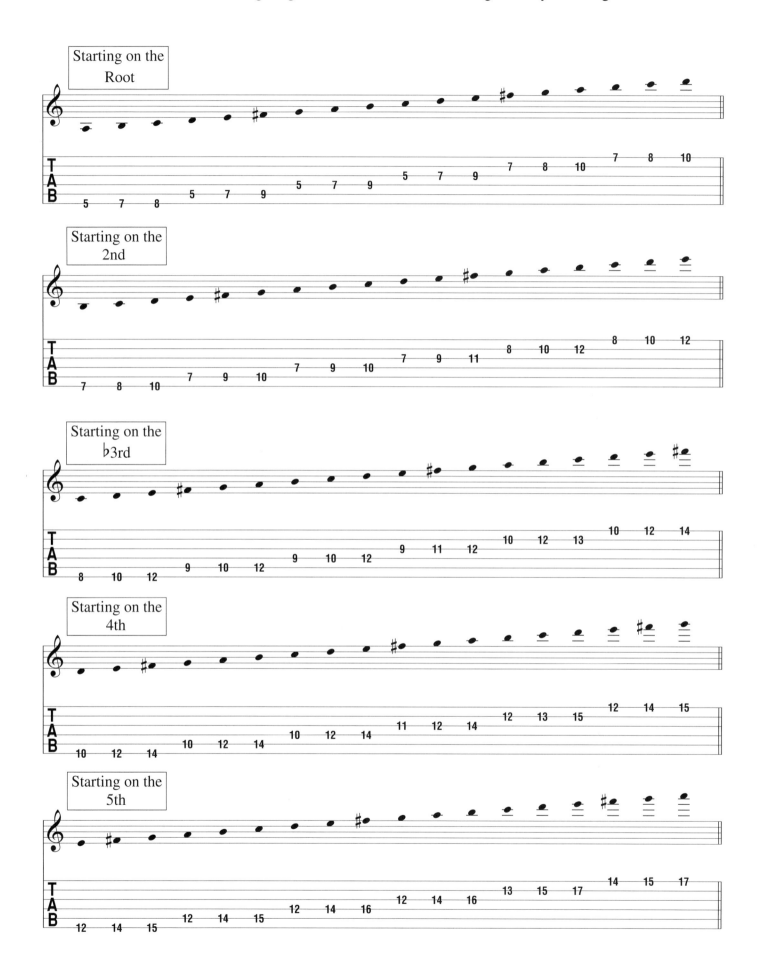

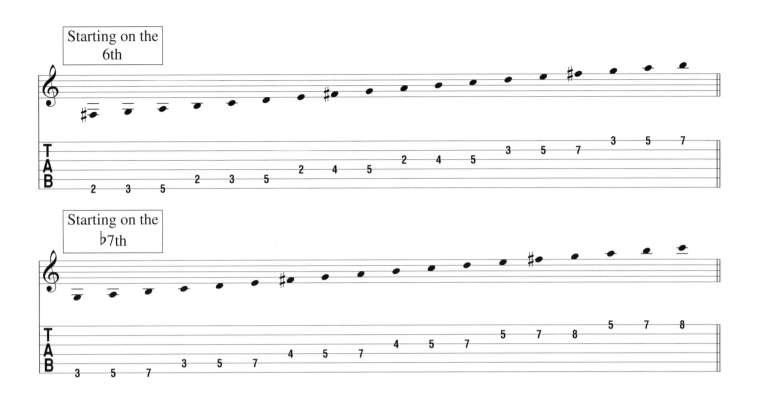

Here are some examples of what Dorian sounds like in a blues fusion context.

The use of the 13th (6th) over minor 7-type chords gives Dorian its signature sound. The other commonly used minor scale, the natural minor (also known as the Aeolian mode), has a ♭13th (♭6th), which gives it more of a classical sound and less of a jazzy flavor. In this example, the 13th is emphasized in measure 3. Try the same lick but with the ♭13th (F, on the high E string, fret 13, rather than fret 14) to hear the difference between the Dorian and Aeolian sounds.

Track 21

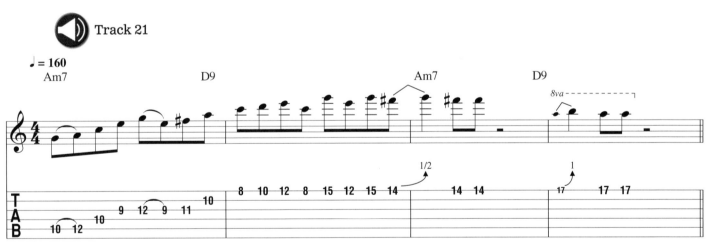

Practice the previous lick against this play-along track. Also practice using A Dorian to come up with your own licks.

Play-Along 11

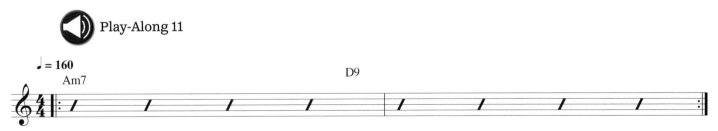

A very common blues fusion move is the arpeggiated run up to the ♭7th of a minor 7 chord arpeggio followed by a fall to the 13th, as heard here in measure 2. Practice this shape and get it under your fingers.

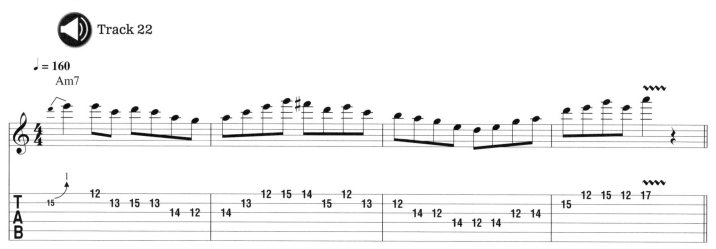

Practice the previous lick against this play-along track.

This next run makes use of 6ths derived from A Dorian. In measure 1, the 6ths are played on adjacent strings, while in measure 2 they're played on the E and G strings.

Use Play-Along 7 again as a backing track for the previous lick. Also practice using A Dorian to come up with your own licks.

This A Dorian lick uses skips and arpeggiated contours to create a line that has more melodic interest than just running up and down the scale. When you create your own lines, try to skip or leave out notes here or there so the line isn't so predictable.

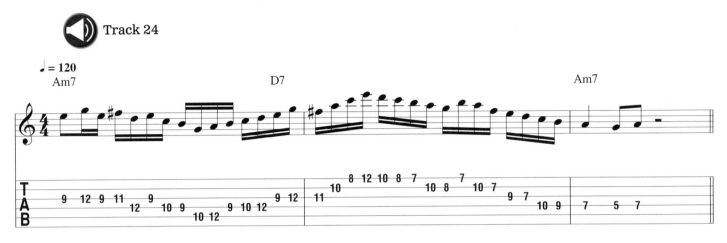

Track 24

Now practice the last lick with this play-along track.

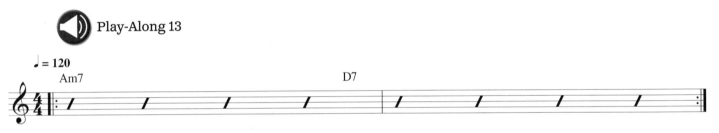

Play-Along 13

Mixolydian: 1–2–3–4–5–6–♭7

The Mixolydian scale is a very common choice for blues fusion and is used over dominant chords. Here are some moveable fingerings for A Mixolydian starting on every scale degree:

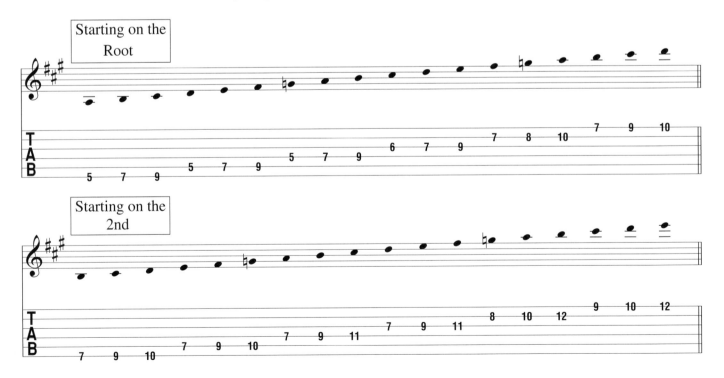

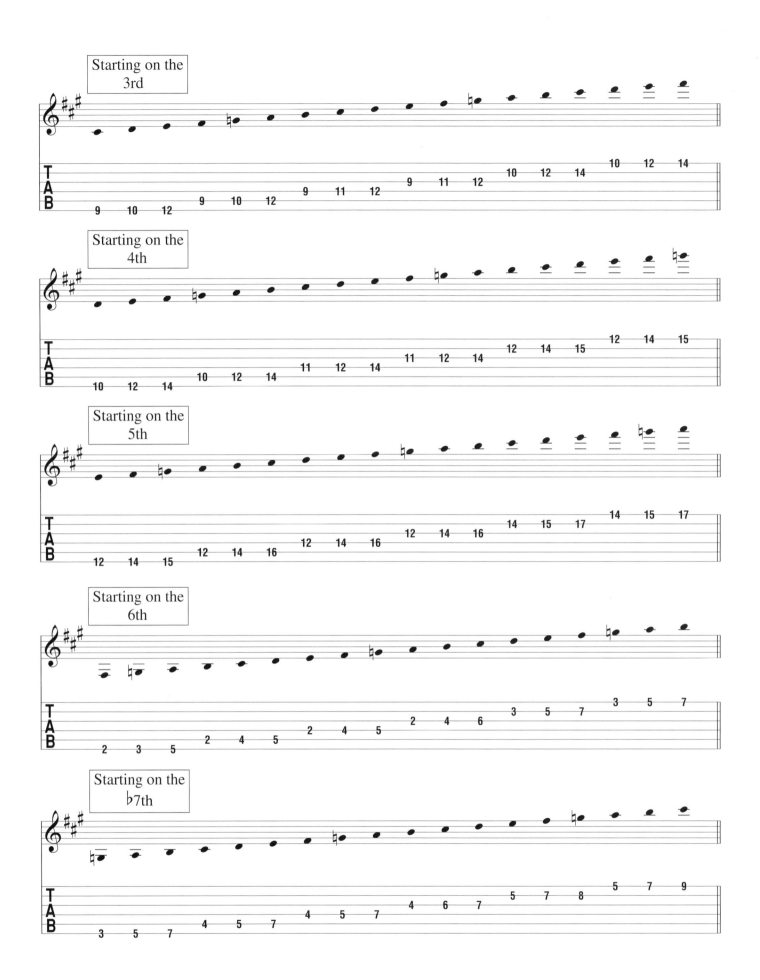

For blues playing, one way of thinking about Mixolydian is that it's like a major pentatonic scale but with added 4th (11th) and ♭7th tones. You'll sometimes hear people refer to the 11th as an "avoid" note because, when held over a dominant 7 chord, it can sound dissonant against the major 3rd. I would suggest taking the "avoid" label with a grain of salt. Just use your ears and decide what works and what doesn't. If it sounds "wrong" when you're holding it, just resolve down a half step to the 3rd. It's certainly a great note to use in passing.

Here are some examples of what Mixolydian sounds like in a blues fusion context. As we saw when we looked at the minor 6 pentatonic scale, the 6th degree can add sweetness to a phrase. This A Mixolydian phrase benefits from the colorful 6th in the pickup measure and then emphasizes the 9th, another colorful note, in measures 1 and 3.

Track 25

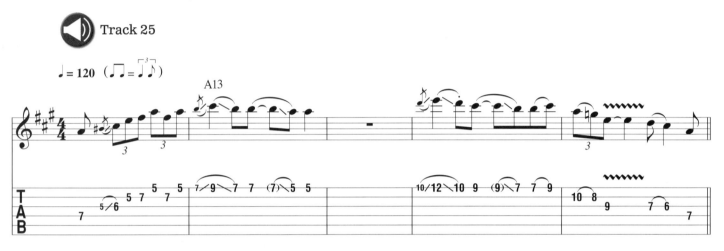

A common Mixolydian move is to bend from the 6th to the ♭7th. The emphasized bends in measures 1 and 2 highlight this and create a yearning, bluesy cry. A descending A7 arpeggio, played as consecutive triplets, rounds out the phrase in measure 4.

Track 26

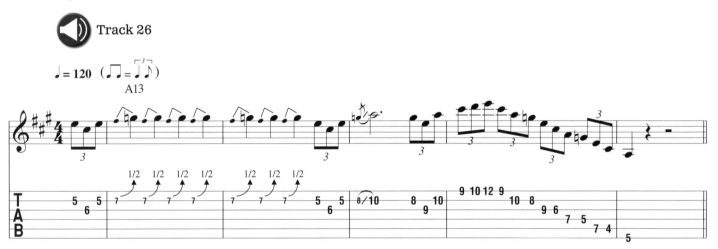

With a few adjustments, Mixolydian can function within a typical minor pentatonic framework because both of these scales share many notes. In this example, the bend from the ♭7th to the root in measure 1 sounds like a common move usually derived from the A minor pentatonic scale. But these notes are also found in A Mixolydian, and here's what can result if you use Mixolydian as a reference.

Track 27

This A Mixolydian line uses string skipping and legato phrasing to achieve a slippery sax-like sound. Even though there are a lot of notes in this phrase, the chord tones are still easily discernible. Note the jump from the 3rd (C♯) to the root (A) on beat 2, measure 1 and beat 1, measure 3 (played an octave lower).

Track 28

Practice the previous licks against this play-along track. Also practice using A Mixolydian to come up with your own licks.

Play-Along 14

ARPEGGIOS

Arpeggios are the notes of a chord played individually—as opposed to simultaneously—and are an important part of the blues fusion player's vocabulary. If you're not too familiar with arpeggios, you might think of them as something that people play really fast up and down the neck. And while that's one common way arpeggios are used, they can also be used melodically. Because an arpeggio contains all the tones of a chord, once you master a fingering, you also learn where the chord tones are located.

Here are fingerings for some essential arpeggios. Use these fingerings as a guideline, but feel free to alter them to suit your own needs. For example, if you want to sweep pick the shapes, you might need to change a fingering to accommodate that technique. The same logic applies if your style incorporates a lot of legato playing. You might then want to change the note locations so that you can hammer on or pull off to certain notes in the shape. Once you learn the shapes, practice them in different rhythms and with different articulations over the backing tracks throughout this book. Then transpose the shapes and try to fit the arpeggio over the new keys.

If you're well versed in music theory and want to try some other arpeggios not listed, feel free to adjust notes accordingly to fit the chord type that you desire.

A Major – A

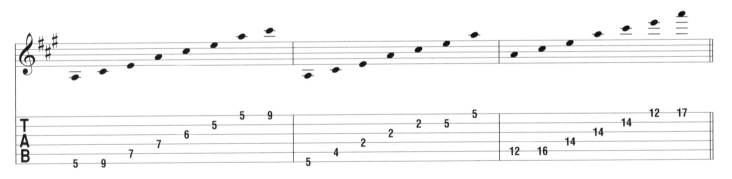

A Minor – Am

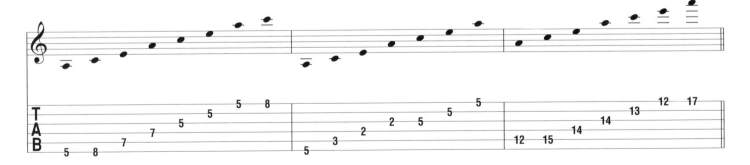

A Diminished – A°

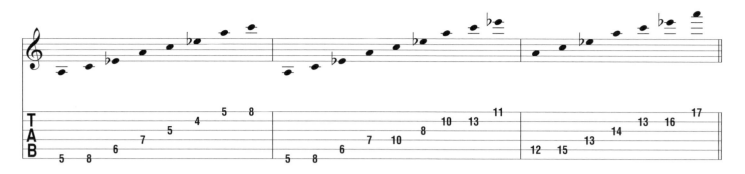

A Augmented – A+

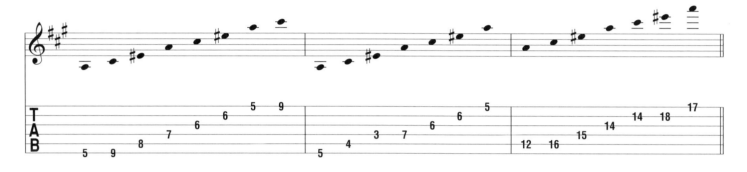

A Major Seven – Amaj7

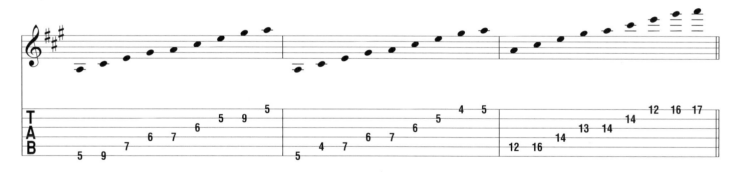

A Minor Seven – Am7

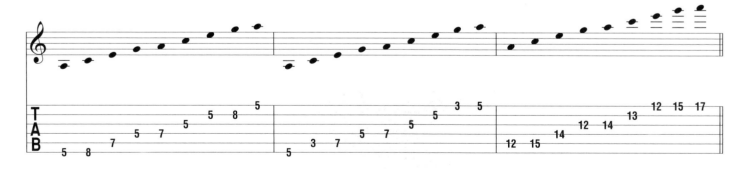

A Seven – A7

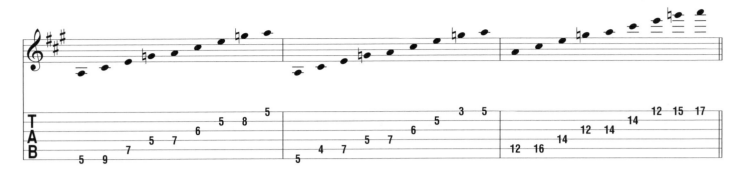

A Minor Seven Flat Five – Am7♭5

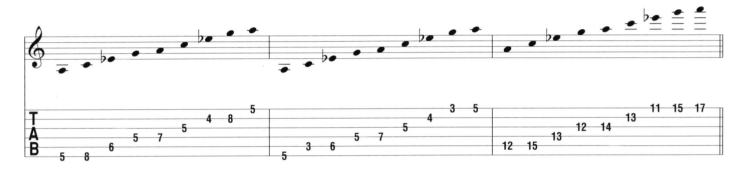

A Major Seven Sharp Five – Amaj7♯5

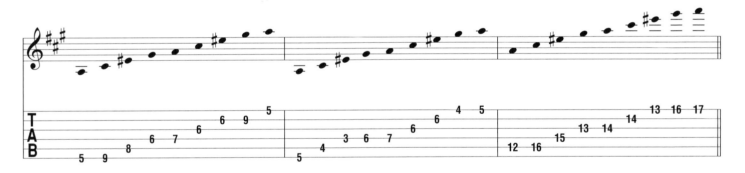

A Minor Major Seven – Am(maj7)

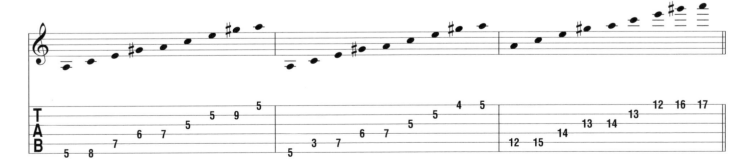

PHRASING CONCEPTS

Now that you've got some scales and arpeggios together, it's time to start improvising with these tools. If you already have experience improvising, these tips should help you tighten up your solos.

Leave Space

One trap musicians sometimes fall into once they achieve technical fluency—especially guitar players—is to feel as though they have to use all of it at every possible opportunity. It's important to remember that all of the devices you've learned, and will continue to learn, are only tools that you have at your disposal. In and of themselves, they don't make music. You have to use the tools to create music in your own way.

In many cases, the phrase "less is more" speaks a valuable truth. If you overplay—no matter how impressive it might be, technically speaking—at some point soon, people in the audience will tune out. Conversely, if you leave space between phrases, when you do go for that hot lick, it will really stick out and grab everyone's attention.

Here's an example of using space as a musical element. After the initial phrase, nothing is played until just before measure 3.

Track 29

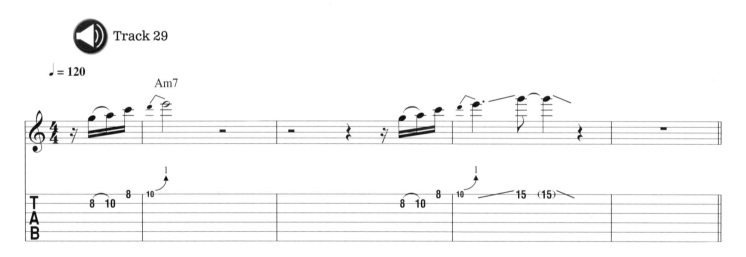

Now create your own example. After you play a short phrase starting around measure 1, wait until around measure 3 to come back in with the next phrase.

Here's another example of using space as a musical gesture. Even though fewer notes are used overall, it still makes for an effective musical statement; it also leaves room to develop ideas and stretch out later in the solo.

Track 30

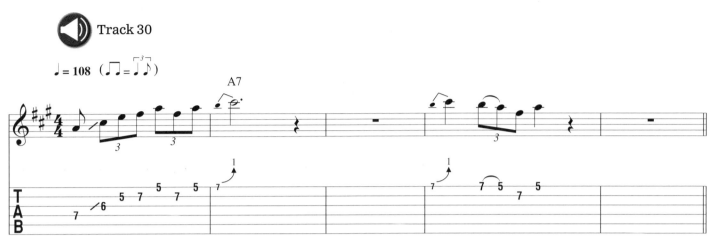

Call and Response

One very common phrasing technique is "call and response," in which a statement is answered by something that logically follows and complements it. Many blues lyrics are naturally set up in a call-and-response format, so you might already be familiar with this concept.

Play through these examples and try coming up with similar, simple phrases that make sense musically.

Track 31

Track 32

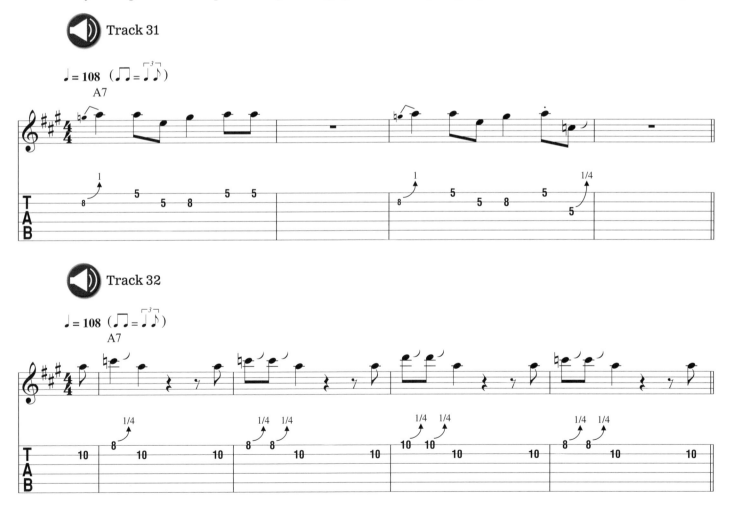

SOLOING OVER CHORD CHANGES

Chord Tones

Hitting *chord tones* over chords is one surefire way to make things sound "good," because every note will be technically "right." If you mastered the arpeggio shapes we just looked at, you should have a good handle on where the chord tones are. When you practice improvising over chord changes, you should ideally be aware of which note you're playing over the chord and how it's functioning.

Here are some exercises to help you become more aware of chord tones as you improvise. The framework will be a V–IV–I progression—the chords for the last four measures of a typical 12-bar blues:

E7	D7	A7		
V	IV	I		

Two fingerings are shown for each example to give you an idea of some options. The displayed fingerings are just a springboard; seek out different fingerings for the same notes. Once you've mastered these exercises, create your own exercises to improve your ability to find chord tones. This is an area of study on which you can spend a lifetime.

Play only the root of each chord as a whole note starting on beat 1:

🔊 Track 33

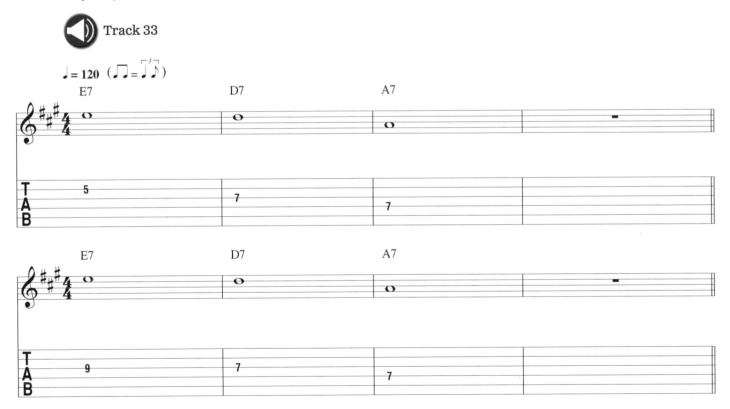

Play only the 3rd of each chord as a whole note starting on beat 1:

Track 34

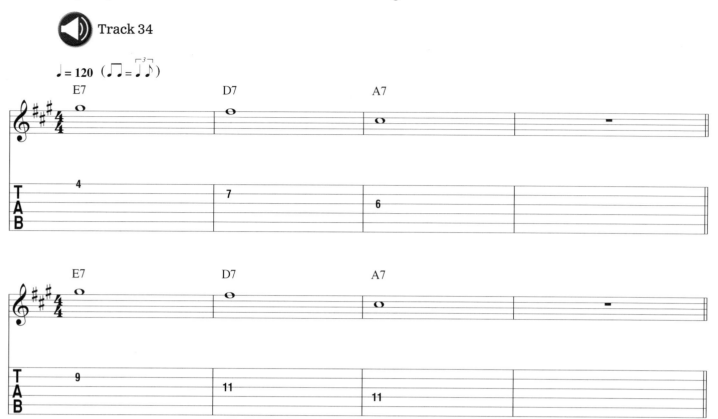

Play only the 5th of each chord as a whole note starting on beat 1:

Track 35

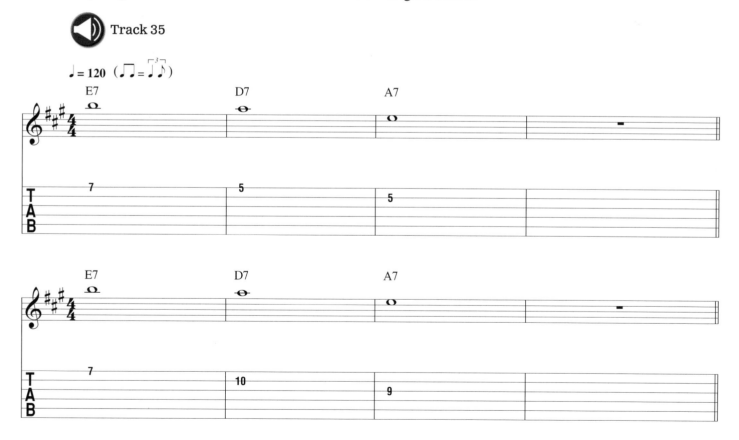

Play only the ♭7th of each chord as a whole note starting on beat 1:

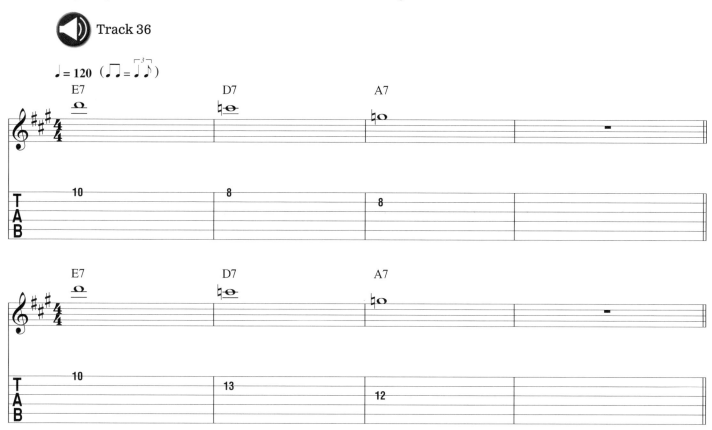

Track 36

Play the root and 3rd of each chord, in half notes, starting on beat 1:

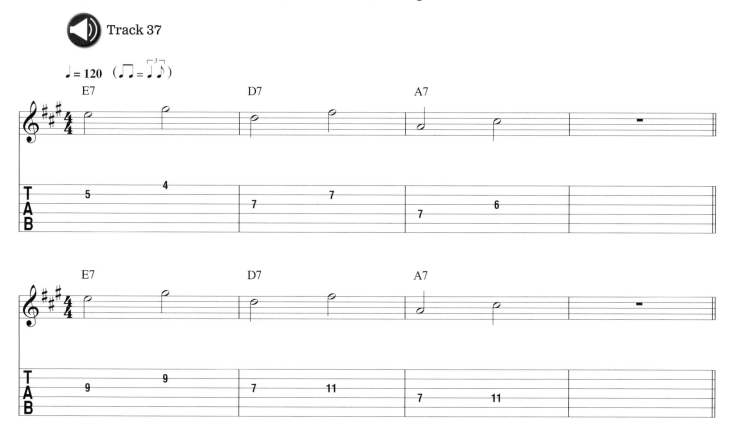

Track 37

Play the 3rd and 5th of each chord, in half notes, starting on beat 1:

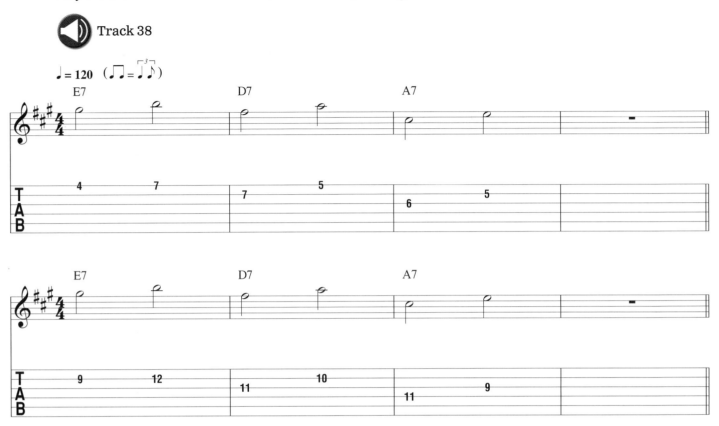

Play the 5th and ♭7th of each chord, in half notes, starting on beat 1:

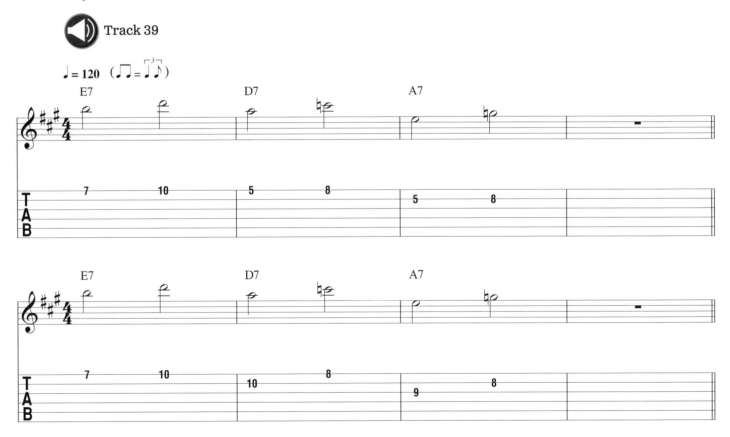

Play the ♭7th and root of each chord, in half notes, starting on beat 1:

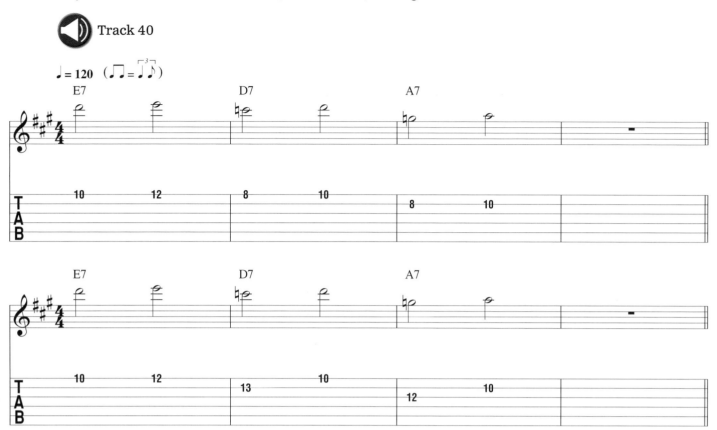

Play the root, 3rd, 5th, and ♭7th of each chord, as quarter notes, starting on beat 1:

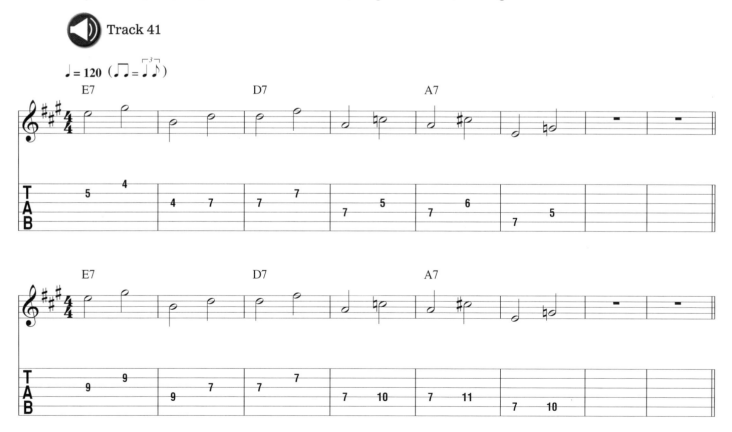

Play the root of each chord and move down to the 3rd, in half notes, starting on beat 1:

Track 42

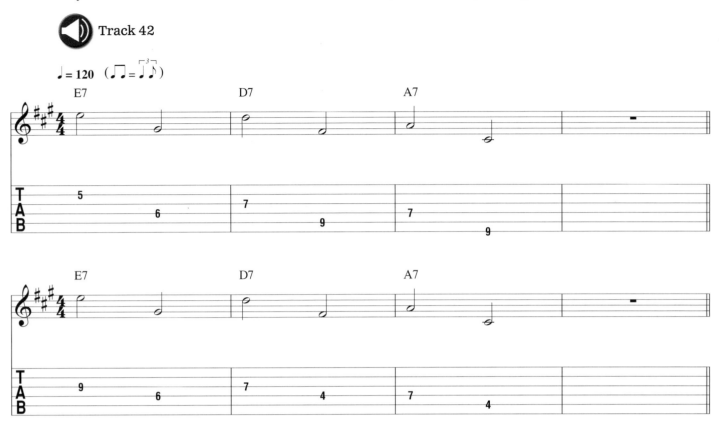

Play the 3rd of each chord and move down to the 5th, in half notes, starting on beat 1:

Track 43

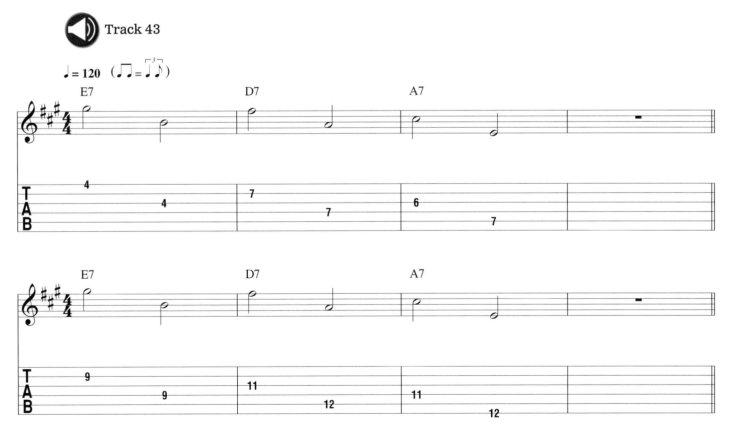

Play the 5th of each chord and move down to the ♭7th, in half notes, starting on beat 1:

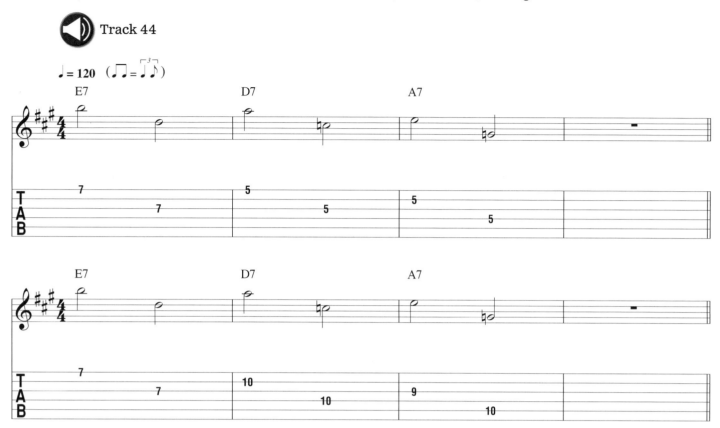

Track 44

Play the ♭7th of each chord and move down to the root, in half notes, starting on beat 1:

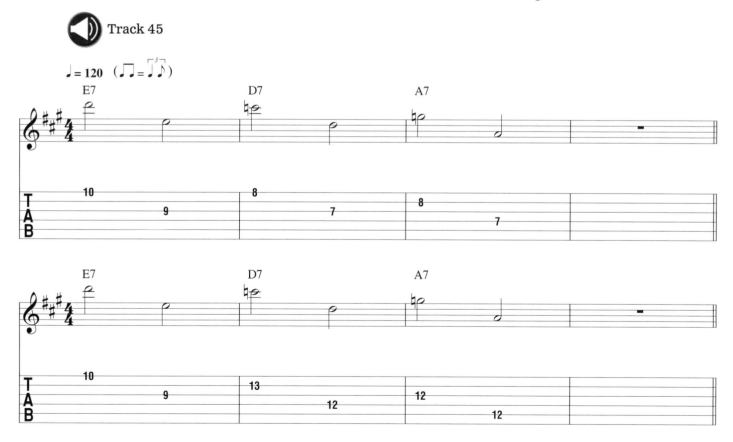

Track 45

Play the root of each chord and move down to the 3rd, up to the 5th, and down to the ♭7th of each chord, in quarter notes, starting on beat 1:

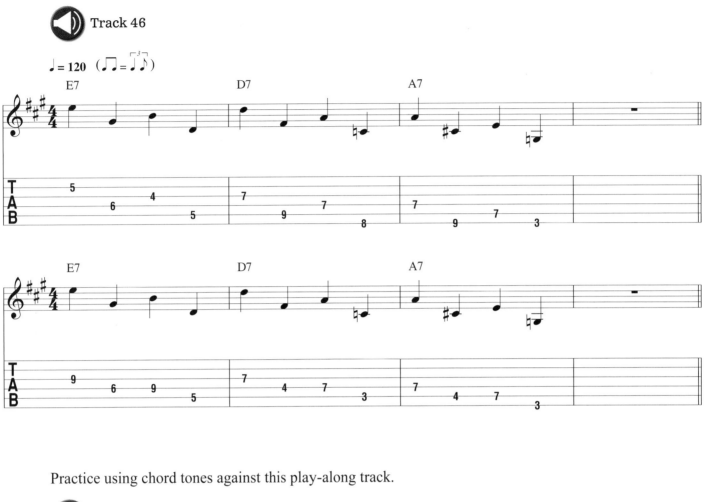

Track 46

Practice using chord tones against this play-along track.

Play-Along 15

Once you have a grasp on where the chord tones are, you can begin to make music with them. Here's an example of a complete 12-bar blues solo played using only chord tones.

Track 47

Mastering chord tones is a very important skill to develop. But a solo that only uses chord tones can get boring pretty quickly. Now that you've learned about chord tones, let's look at ways of integrating other notes to create interesting lines.

When you use notes exclusively from a scale, the term for that is *diatonic*. On the other hand, notes that are not part of the key are known as *chromatic*. A good mix of diatonic and chromatic material can create some really cool blues fusion lines. Here are some ways to integrate diatonic and chromatic material with the chord tones you just worked on.

Passing Tones

Passing tones are scale tones inserted between chord tones (they can also be notes inserted between scale tones) and fall into two categories: diatonic and chromatic. Diatonic passing tones occur naturally in the key, whereas chromatic passing tones do not belong to the key and are inserted either between chord or scale tones.

If this concept is new to you, one easy way to get started is to physically fill in the holes between the A minor pentatonic shape by playing every fret within the outer fingers.

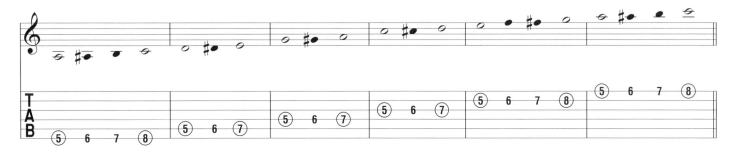

Here are the diatonic passing tones within an A7 arpeggio. These notes are derived from A Mixolydian.

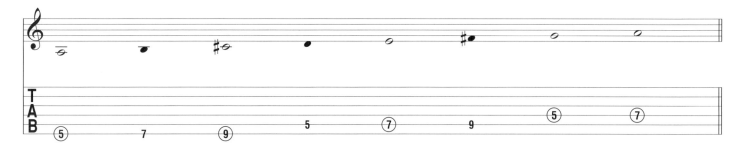

And here are both diatonic and chromatic passing tones within an A7 arpeggio. A Mixolydian is the reference scale here, although with everything filled in, you might notice that the result is a chromatic scale from A to A. While that may be the case, it's important for you to be aware of which notes are chord tones, diatonic passing tones, and chromatic passing tones.

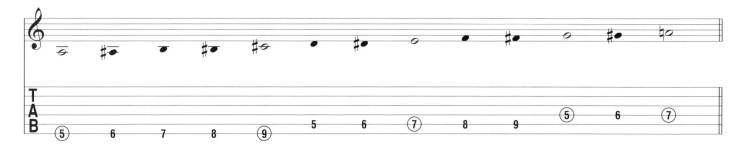

Neighbor Tones

Neighbor tones are the notes located directly above or below a chord or scale tone. After a neighbor tone, or a series of neighbor tones, the adjacent chord or scale tone needs to be played for a complete resolution. Like passing tones, neighbor tones can be either diatonic or chromatic. Generally, chromatic neighbor notes will resolve into chord tones or the nearest scale tone.

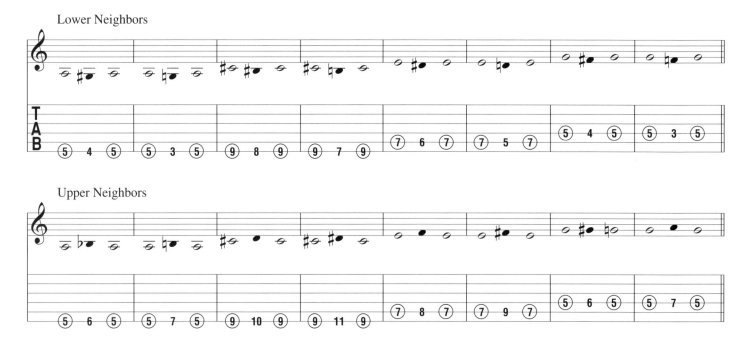

Surround Tones

You can use upper and lower neighbors in combination to "surround" a note. These are referred to as *surround tones* and can consist of both diatonic and chromatic neighbors. Using surround tones, virtually all the notes of the chromatic scale can be accessed and neatly resolved. You'll sometimes hear great players use a lot of chromatic notes, but if you listen carefully, you'll hear that it's not random. There's a hidden strategy at work.

Here, the notes of A7 are surrounded by diatonic upper and lower neigbors in A Mixolydian.

Here, the notes of A7 are surrounded by diatonic upper and either chromatic or diatonic lower neighbors (whichever produces a half step below the target note) in A Mixolydian.

When you combine all of these approaches, you can get a lot of movement. This A7 line gets some nice chromaticism by surrounding the root and later the 5th.

🔊 Track 48

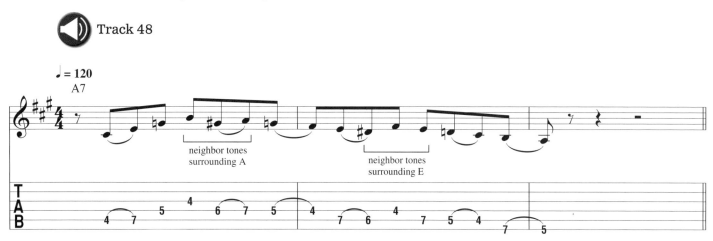

This line mixes passing tones and surround tones to get a ton of chromatics that all perfectly resolve.

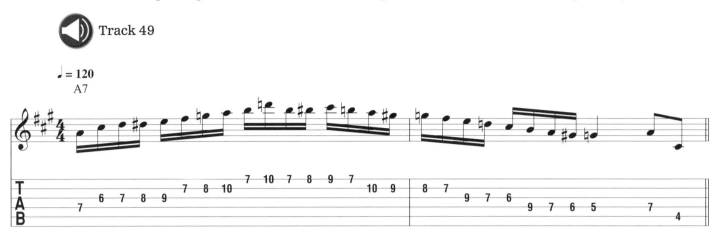

Track 49

Appoggiatura

An *appoggiatura* is a non-chord or scale tone that is approached by a leap and then resolved by step in the opposite direction of the leap.

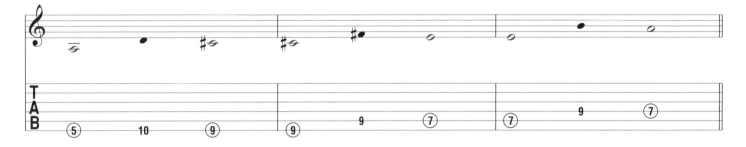

CHORD EXTENSIONS AND ALTERATIONS

So far, we've covered triads (three-note chords) and seventh chords. But you've probably heard of ninth and 13th chords also. Here's what they are all about.

When labeling and describing chords, the notes past the octave—normally the 2nd, 4th, and 6th degrees—are referred to as the 9th, 11th, and 13th. These notes function as *chord extensions* and can be added to any of the seventh chord types we looked at for extra color. The extensions don't change the basic quality of the chord, but they do add color to the overall sound of a scale or chord. A 13th chord is just a more colorful version of a dominant 7 chord; a minor ninth chord is just an elaborate version of a minor seventh chord, etc. Alterations are chromatic changes made to either chord tones or extensions.

Although the system of naming chords isn't completely standardized, complex chords are usually named in the following order: root, quality, and uppermost extension (C13, for example). Altered notes are mentioned last (C13♭9, for example).

In most cases on guitar, not all of the notes that are theoretically possible are actually played simultaneously in a chord voicing. But whether all, only a few, or none of the possible chord extensions are played at a given moment, it is understood that they are available options to choose from depending on the color desired.

Here are some "must-know" chord shapes with extensions and alterations.

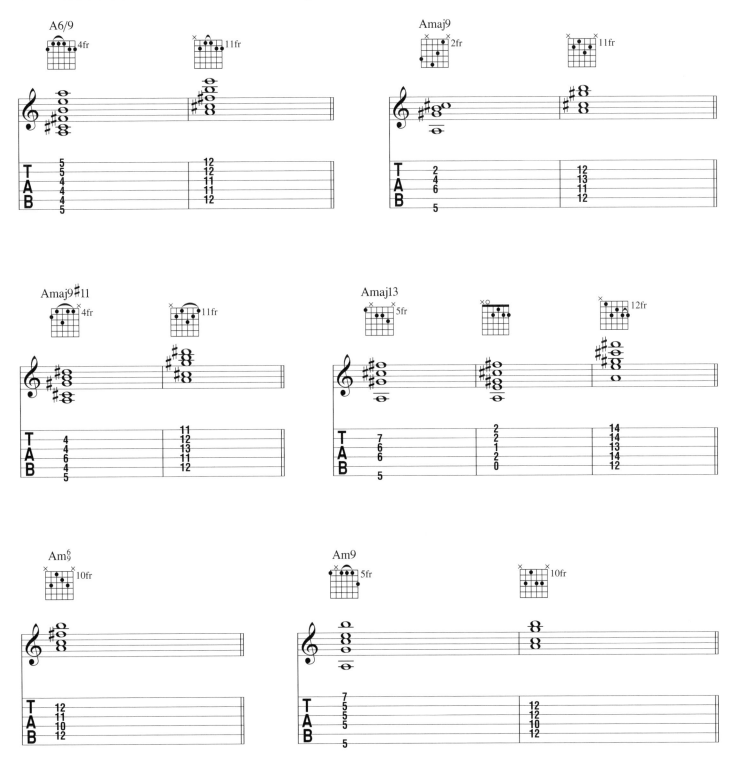

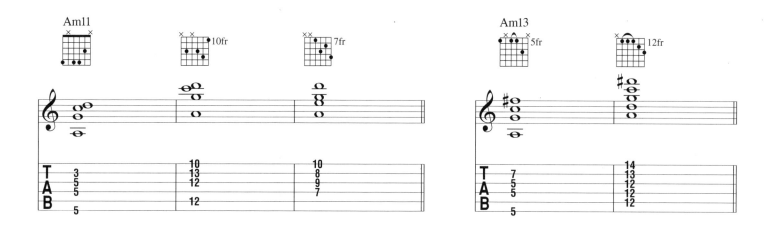

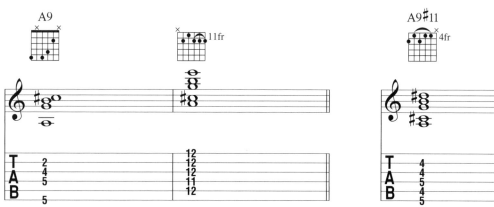

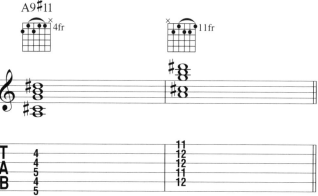

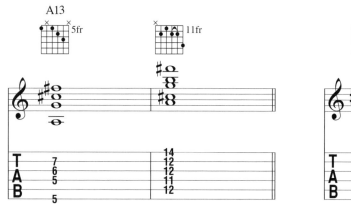

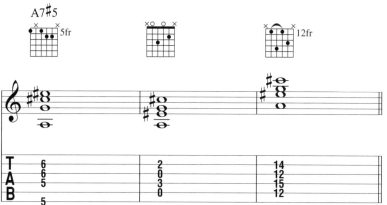

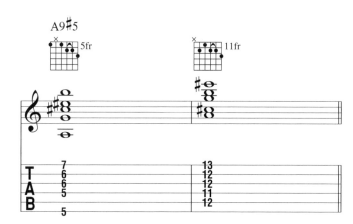

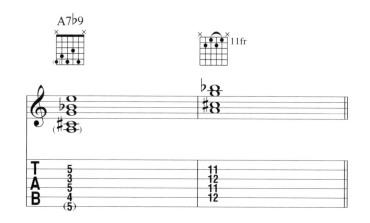

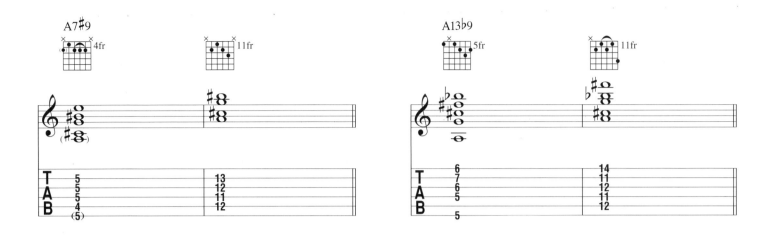

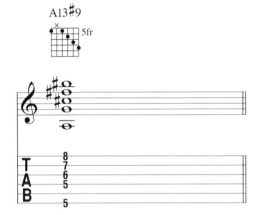

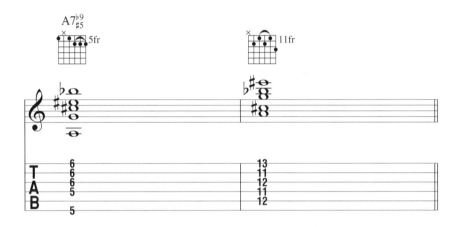

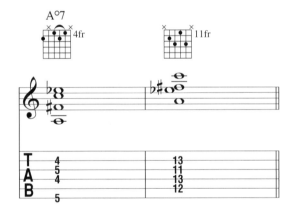

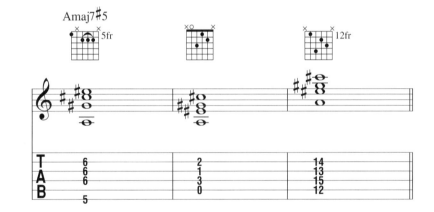

Here's a blues progression in A that includes 13th chords.

Many times chords are played on just the upper strings for a crisper or leaner sound. These types of shapes will often not have the chord's root in the bass, but that's okay because the bass player will likely be playing the root in his bass line. Here are some useful shapes to learn:

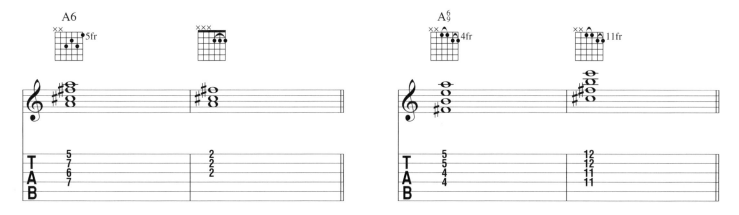

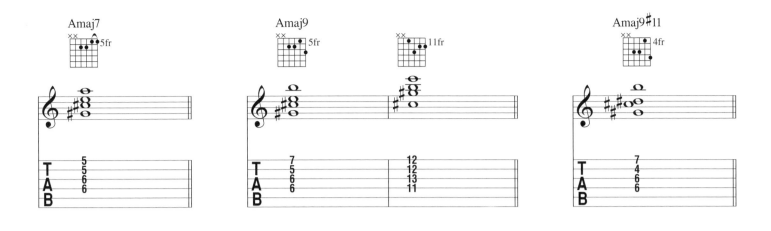

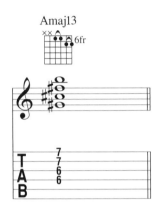
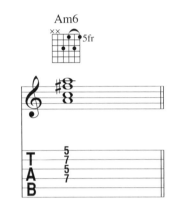
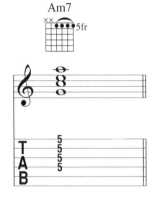
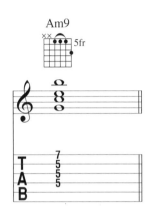

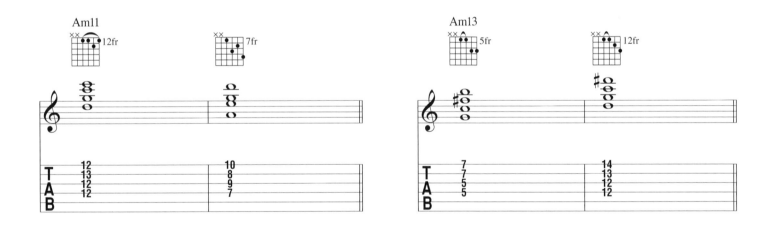

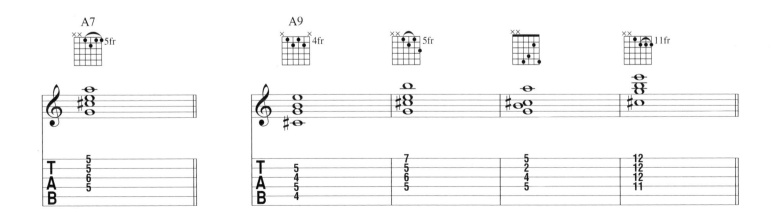

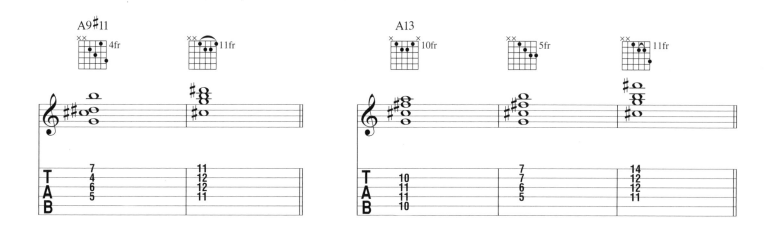

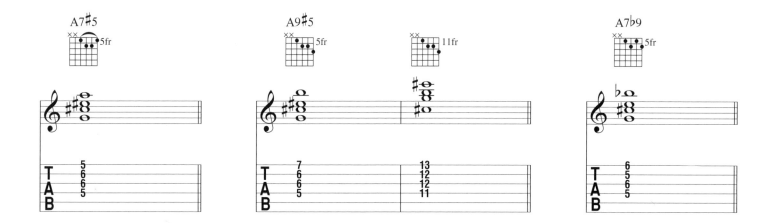

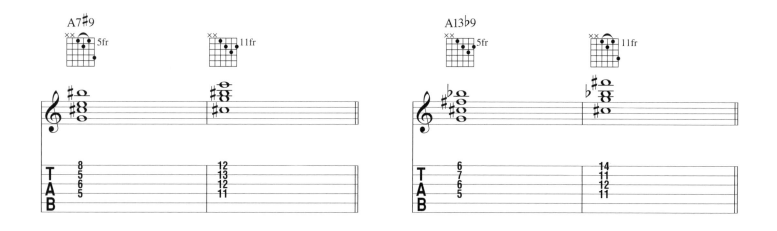

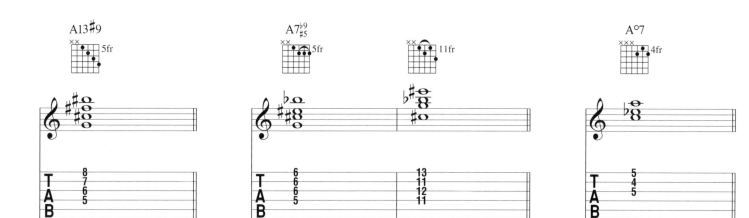

Here are examples of how to use these more concise chord voicings over the 12-bar blues and 12-bar minor blues progressions.

A Minor Blues

Track 51

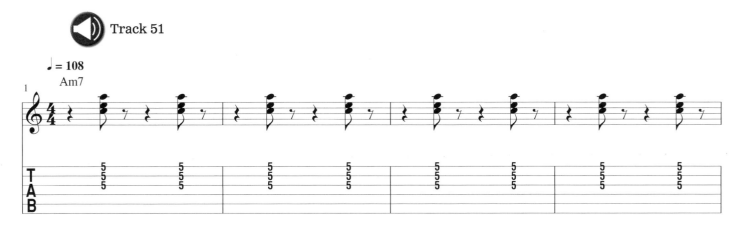

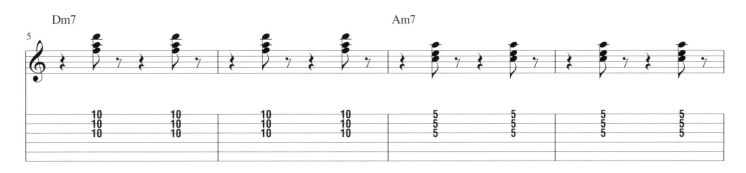

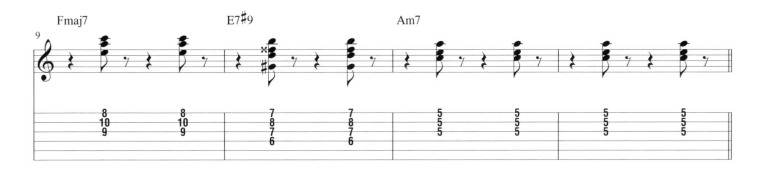

A Blues

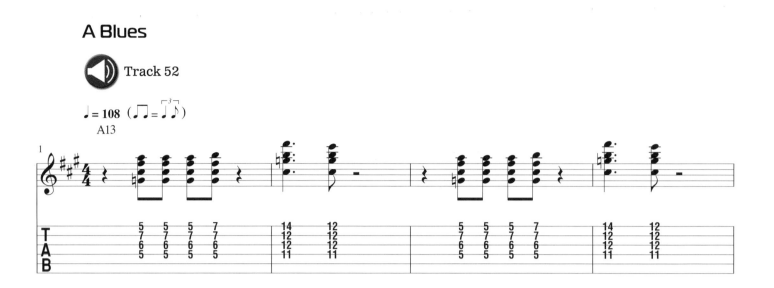

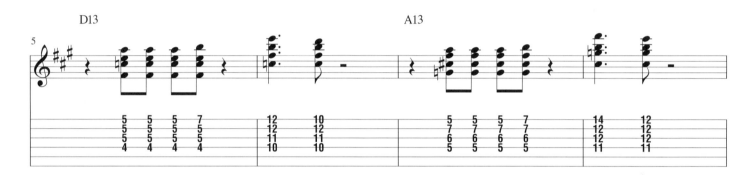

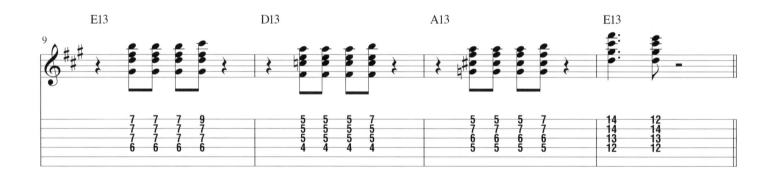

A Blues

Track 53

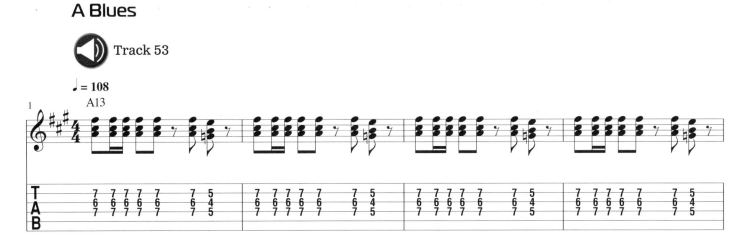

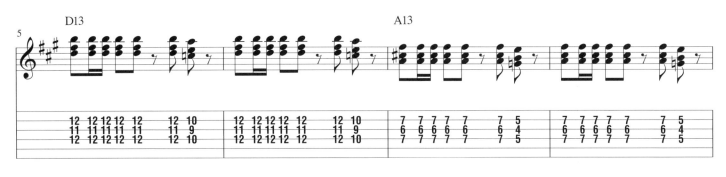

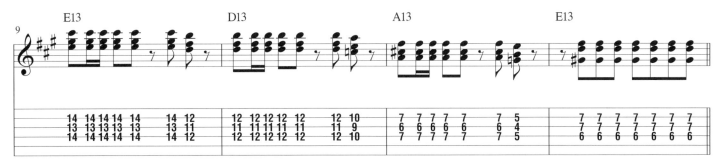

ESSENTIAL ADVANCED SCALES

Many of the great blues fusion players incorporate harmonically sophisticated jazz sonorities into their vocabulary. These sounds are drawn from scales that contain a good amount of tension. Some common choices include the Lydian Dominant, Super Locrian, and half-whole diminished scales.

Lydian Dominant: 1–2–3–♯4–5–6–♭7

Lydian Dominant is used over unaltered dominant chords with a ♯11th. It's also a great choice for just a 9th or 13th chord with no 11th present.

Here are some moveable fingerings for the A Lydian Dominant scale starting on every scale degree:

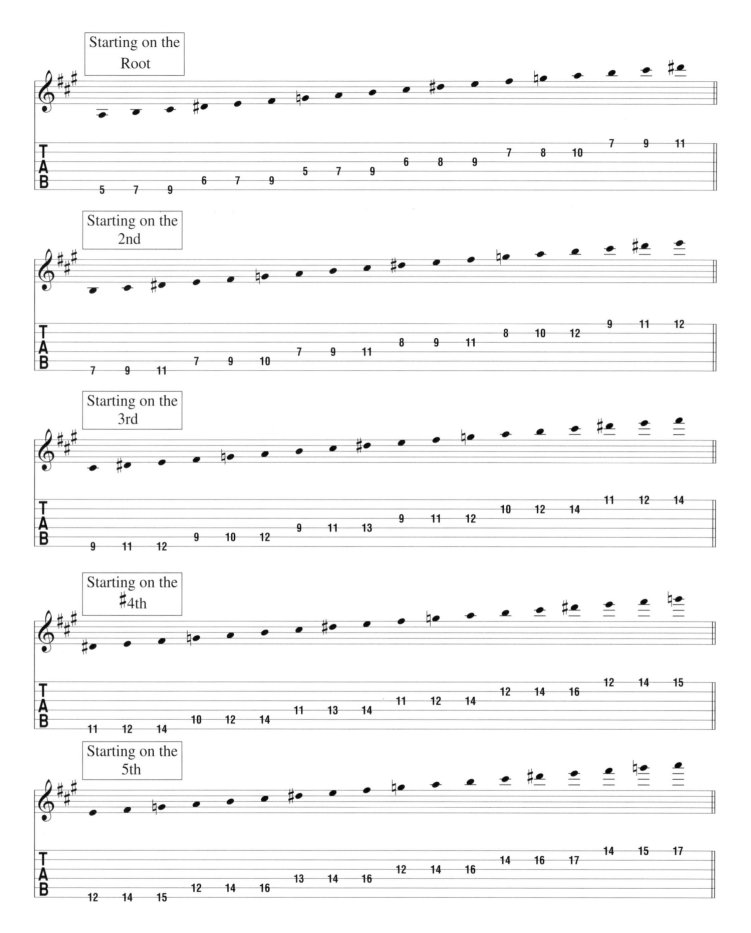

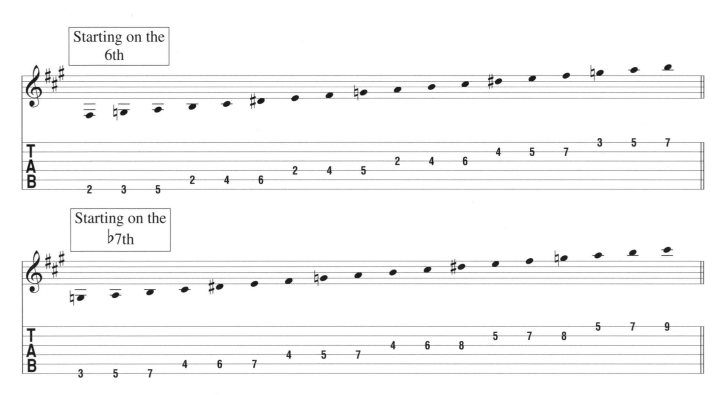

For blues playing, one way of thinking about the Lydian Dominant scale is that it's like a major pentatonic scale with added ♯4th (♯11th) and ♭7th tones. Here are some examples of what the Lydian Dominant scale sounds like in a blues fusion context.

A good way to "sneak in" more advanced scales is to ground your lines with more traditional-sounding licks first. This example uses conventional blues phrasing at first to set up a familiar sound before introducing the Lydian Dominant's distinct ♯11th note at the end of measure 2.

Track 54

♩ = 100

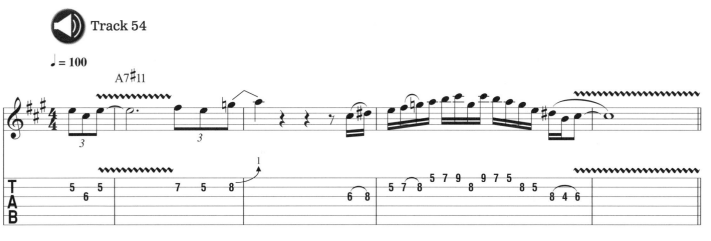

This lick uses legato phrasing to achieve a sax-like sound. Pay close attention to the articulation marks, hammering on and pulling off when noted.

Track 55

♩ = 100

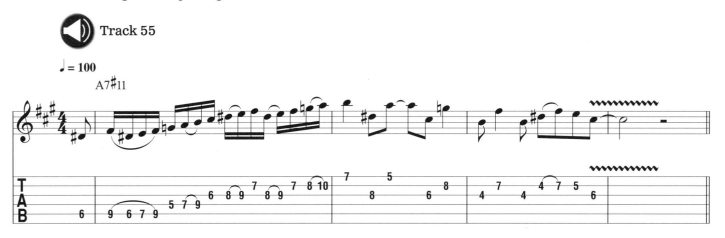

Using repetitive licks can help build momentum and energy. This lick starts with a three-note repeating motive that, through rhythmic manipulation, becomes a three-against-four hemiola starting on beat 3 of measure 1, until beat 1 of measure 2. For more information on manipulating rhythm, check out the "Rhythmic Ideas for Soloing" chapter on page 78.

Track 56

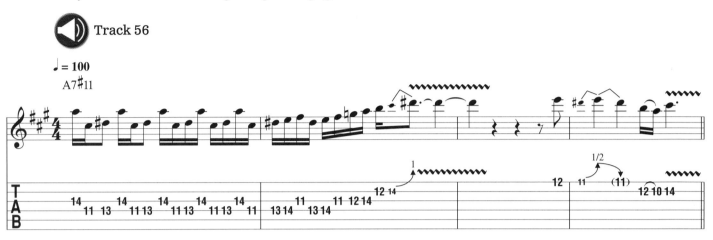

One way to make the Lydian Dominant's pungent ♯11th less jarring is to bend it up to the 5th, as done here, starting on beat 4 of measure 1. Bending out of dissonant notes into consonant ones is a good way to integrate less common tensions.

Track 57

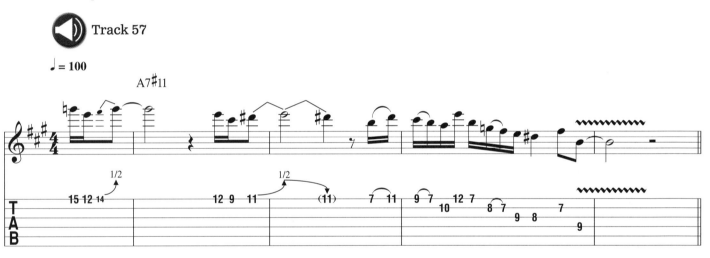

Practice the previous licks against this play-along track. Also practice using A Lydian Dominant to come up with your own licks.

Play-Along 16

For playing over chords with ♭9th, ♯9th, or ♯11th tensions, the Super Locrian and half-whole diminished scales are very common choices. The distinction between the two scales is that Super Locrian has a ♭13th, so it's a great choice for an altered chord with a ♭13th. The half-whole diminished scale has a natural 13th, however, which makes it a great choice for any 13th chord with an altered 9th or 11th.

Super Locrian: 1–♭2–♯2–3–♯4–♯5–♭7

Here are some moveable fingerings for A Super Locrian starting on every scale degree:

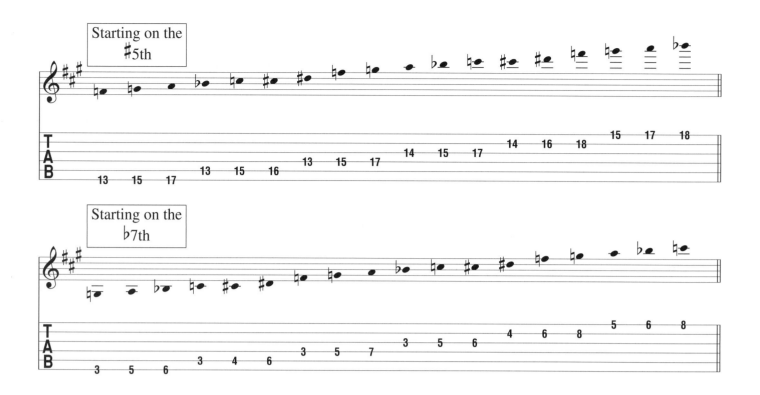

Here are some examples of what Super Locrian sounds like in a blues fusion context.

Super Locrian can also be thought of as the seventh mode of melodic minor (see the chart at the end of this chapter for more information on the melodic minor scale). Oftentimes, when improvisers see an altered chord with a ♭13th, they'll think of playing the melodic minor scale up a half step from the root of the chord. This lick is a cliché that jazz players have played for years. Here, it's based on B♭ melodic minor over A7alt.

🔊 Track 58

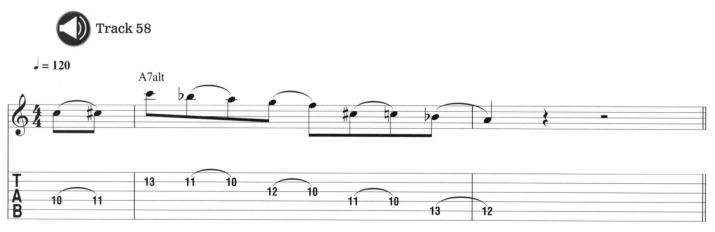

An interesting thing is that from the major 3rd up to the root in the altered scale, it's all whole steps. This can imply a whole tone scale sound (see the chart at the end of this chapter for more information on the whole tone scale). For this reason, this scale is sometimes called half diminished/half whole tone. From measure 1 up to beat 2 of measure 2, this lick toys around with a whole tone tonality before adding in the other notes of A Super Locrian.

Track 59

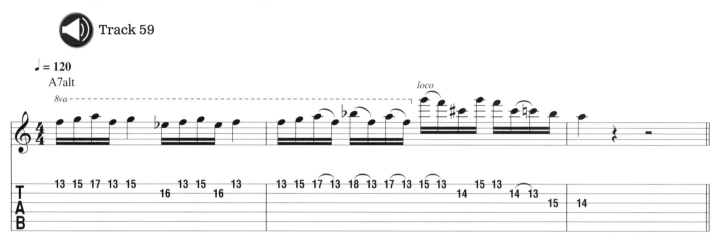

Jazz players often use a 1–2–3–5 Coltrane-influenced pattern in their lines. In the Super Locrian scale, we can build 1–2–3–5 patterns starting on the #4th and #5th (D# and E#, respectively, from A altered). In this lick, these shapes serve as the basis for the repeating lick from measure 1 to measure 2, beat 2, respectively. In the notation, enharmonic equivalent spellings are used (1–2–3–5 built on E♭ and F) for ease of reading.

Track 60

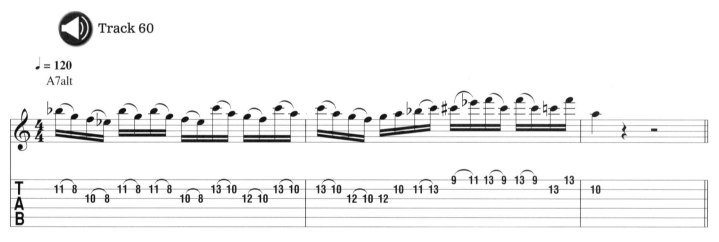

This next phrase mixes serpentine A Super Locrian shapes with ideas based on B♭ melodic minor (similar to the first example in this section) in measure 2 (although played here at a faster speed).

Track 61

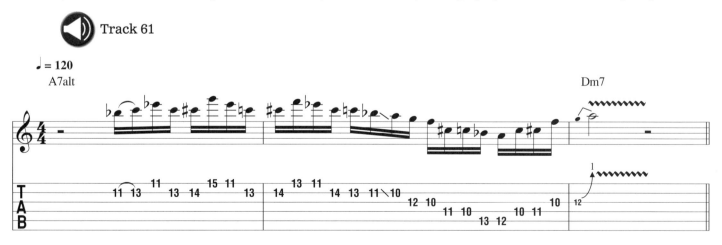

Practice the previous licks against this play-along track. Also practice using A Super Locrian to come up with your own licks.

Play-Along 17

♩ = 120

Half-Whole Diminished: 1–♭2–♯2–3–♯4–5–6–♭7

Here are some moveable fingerings for the A half-whole diminished scale. Note that, because the scale is symmetrical, the initial two fingerings are repeated over and over again in minor 3rd intervals:

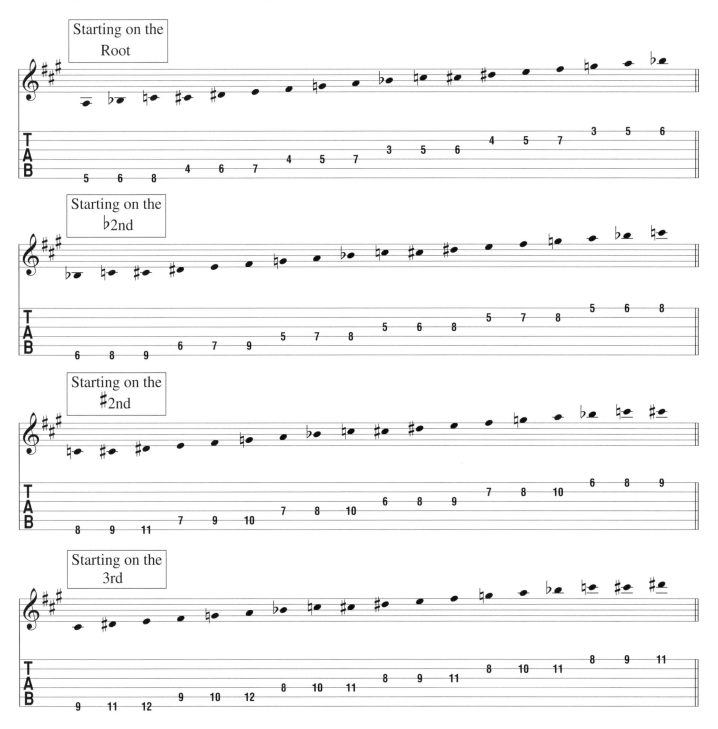

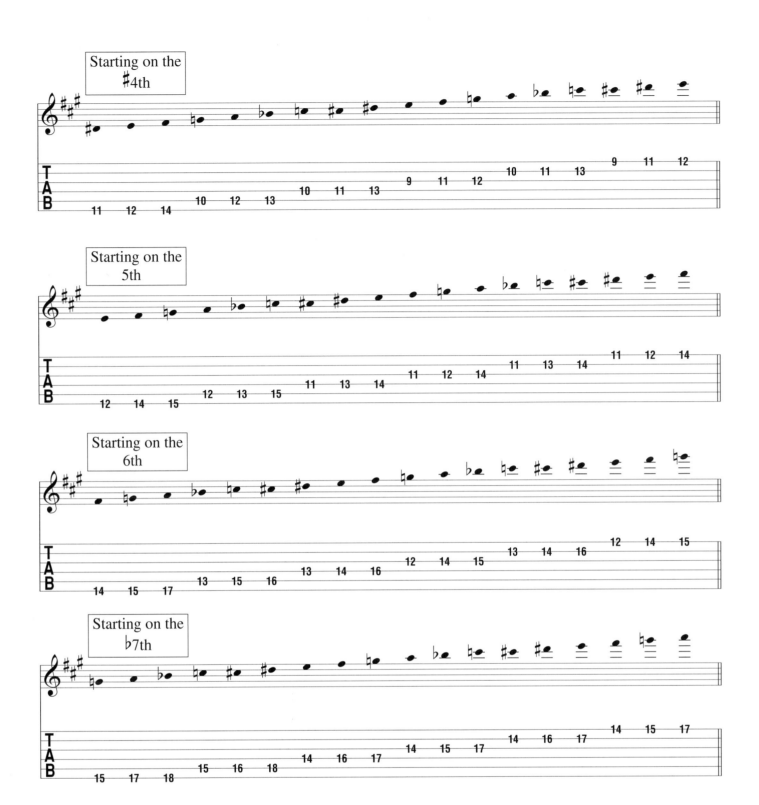

Here are some examples of what the half-whole diminished scale sounds like in a blues fusion context.

From measure 1, beat 2 until beat 2 1/2 of measure 2, the phrase consists of just running up and down the scale. What makes it sound like music as opposed to just "practicing" are the twists and turns that bookend the phrase.

Track 62

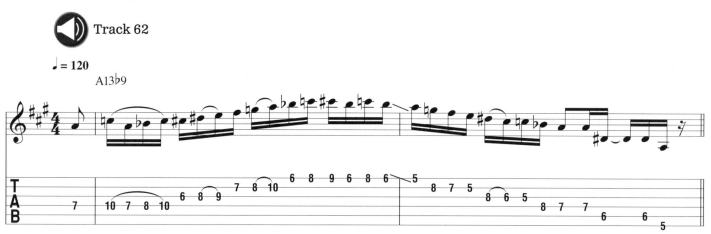

As we looked at in some earlier examples, a good way to "sneak in" more dissonant scales is to start the phrase off with something that sounds more familiar. This next line begins with a straightforward idea that could just as easily come from the A minor pentatonic scale. The A half-whole diminished scale is introduced at the end of beat 2 in measure 2.

Track 63

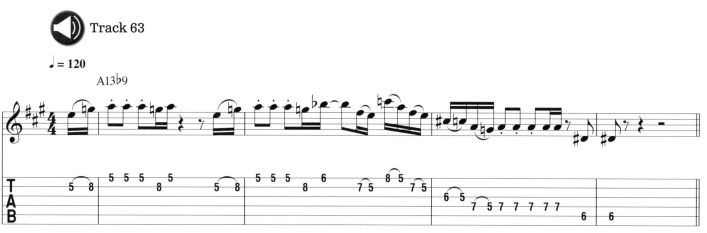

The half-whole diminished scale is also a great source for symmetrical shapes. There are countless possibilities that you can spend a lifetime working on. Here's a common shape based on triads with both major and minor 3rds moving down in minor 3rds.

Track 64

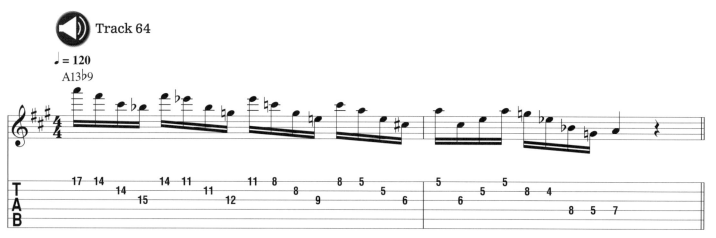

While the half-whole diminished scale contains many tension notes, if you use catchy motives when you phrase with it, you can disguise the dissonances. Note how the call-and-response idea in this phrase grounds the line and makes the long tension-filled passage in measure 3 less conspicuous.

🔊 Track 65

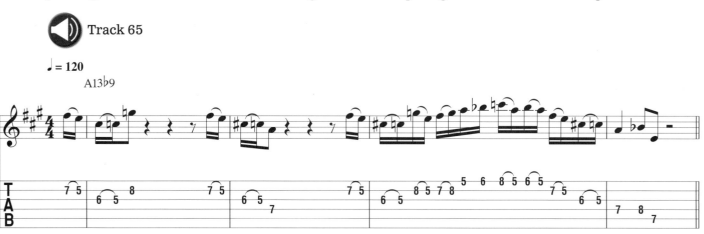

Practice the previous licks against this play-along track. Also practice using A half-whole diminished to come up with your own licks.

🔊 Play-Along 18

More Scales

In addition to the scales we've looked at, there are several more common ones with which you should be familiar. Here's a list with formulas for you to work out on your own. Experiment and create your own licks!

Scale	Formula
Harmonic Minor	1 2 ♭3 4 5 ♭6 7
Melodic Minor	1 2 ♭3 4 5 6 7
Dorian ♭2	1 ♭2 ♭3 4 5 6 ♭7
Lydian Augmented	1 2 3 ♯4 ♯5 6 7
Mixolydian ♭6 (Hindu)	1 2 3 4 5 ♭6 ♭7
Locrian ♮2	1 2 ♭3 4 ♭5 ♭6 ♭7
Whole Tone	1 2 3 ♯4 ♯5 ♭7
Diminished-whole/half	1 2 ♭3 4 ♯4 ♯5 6 7

SCALE AND ARPEGGIO SEQUENCES

A *sequence* is a small, melodic fragment that moves through a scale or arpeggio in a predictable pattern. When you hear players like Joe Bonamassa and Eric Johnson play their impressive, fast lines, sometimes they are simply running through sequences. Here are some shapes to get you going. Practice the sequences from beginning to end so you can get them under your fingers, but keep in mind that, in an actual performance, you'll likely only use a small portion of the sequence (otherwise it could sound too mechanical).

Here's a pattern from the fifth-position A minor pentatonic scale. It starts on the eighth fret of the high E string and descends in groups of four, starting on every note of the minor pentatonic scale.

Track 66

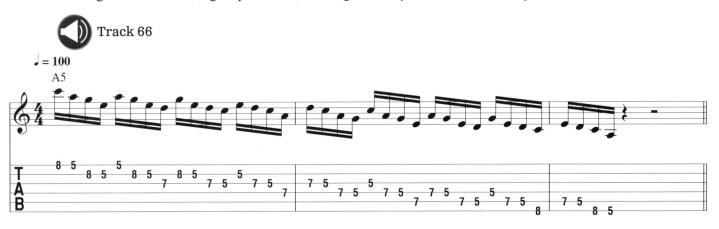

This pattern is the mirror image of the previous one. It ascends in groups of four, starting from the fifth fret of the low E string.

Track 67

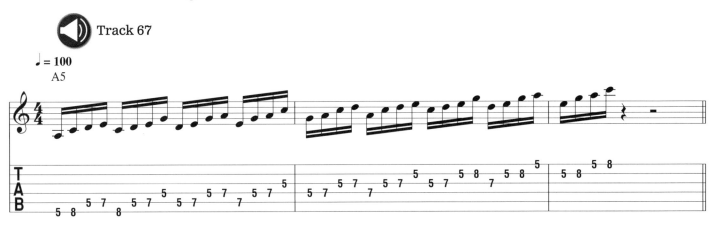

Here's a descending six-note shape similar to something Eric Johnson might play. This shape goes down six notes starting on the high E string and then repeats the shape starting on the B, G, and D strings, respectively.

Track 68

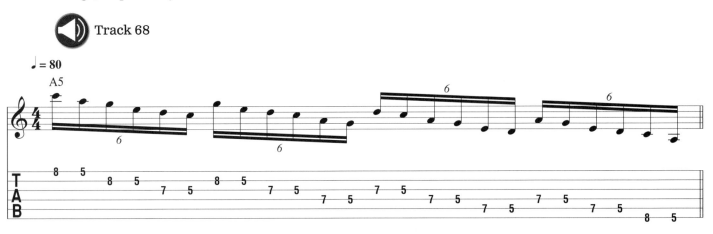

Here's an ascending version of the previous six-note shape. You'll hear Joe Bonamassa do this type of thing as well.

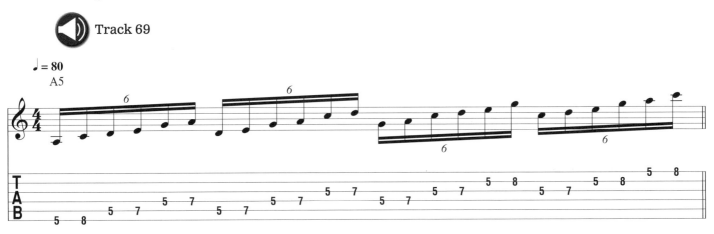

Sequences can also be created from arpeggios. Here we'll take the same concepts behind the descending and ascending patterns we just looked at and apply them to some arpeggios.

Major 7 Arpeggio Sequences

Minor 7 Arpeggio Sequences

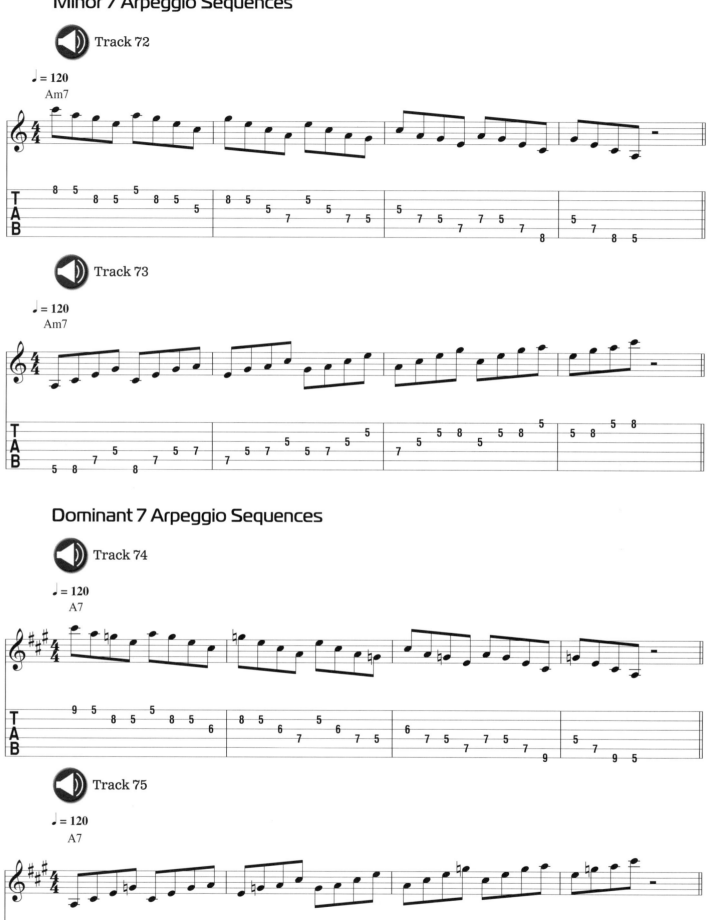

Dominant 7 Arpeggio Sequences

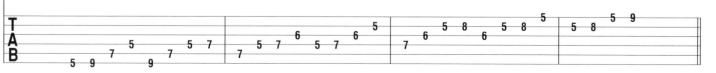

Minor 7♭5 Arpeggio Sequences

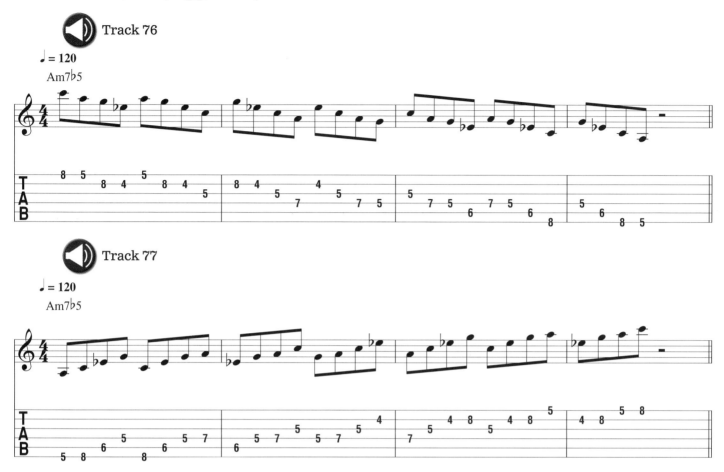

 (continued)

The sequences we looked at were fairly simple in structure but offer a lot of material to work with. Try to create your own sequences. Depending on how you work and process information, it might help to map things out on paper first before applying it to the instrument.

RHYTHMIC IDEAS FOR SOLOING

The sequences we just looked at in the last chapter can generate a lot of excitement from their velocity and steady stream of notes. Another way of generating intensity, however, is to use rhythm to create tension. You can manipulate the rhythms of your phrases to imply different meters that temporarily "fight" or "rub against" the underlying meter. Of course, you'll want to make sure you resolve the phrase in a logical place so it sounds intentional.

Here are some common moves. Playing consecutive dotted half notes in 4/4 will give you an accent every three eighth notes and create the illusion of a 3/8 meter.

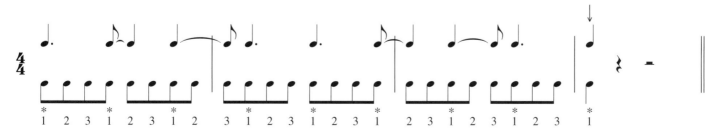

Here's what that sounds like in a musical context.

Track 78

Within the framework of the superimposed rhythm, you can also use other rhythms. Using the previous lick, for example, you don't have to just play dotted quarter notes. The dotted quarter note pattern there is just a frame within which to work. You can still improvise other rhythms freely within; just be mindful of where you are—both in the actual meter and the superimposed meter.

Here's an example of a three-beat framework filled up rhythmically and superimposed against a 4/4 meter. The superimposition occurs between measures 1–3.

Track 79

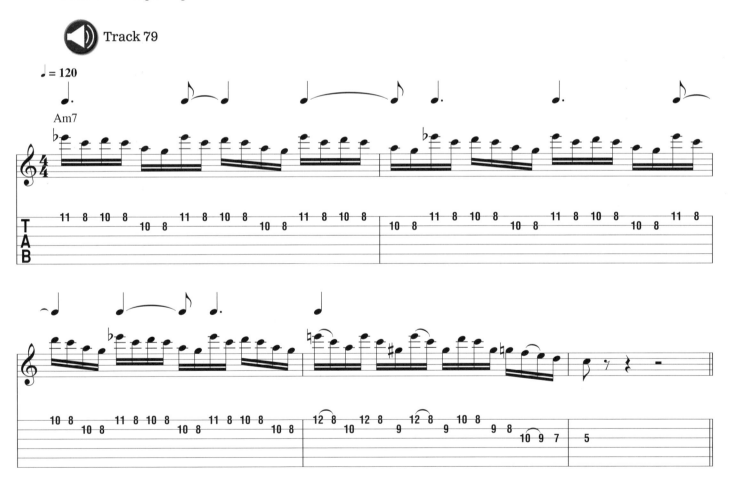

There are endless odd-against-even or even-against-odd groupings possible. Here's a five-against-four rhythmic framework:

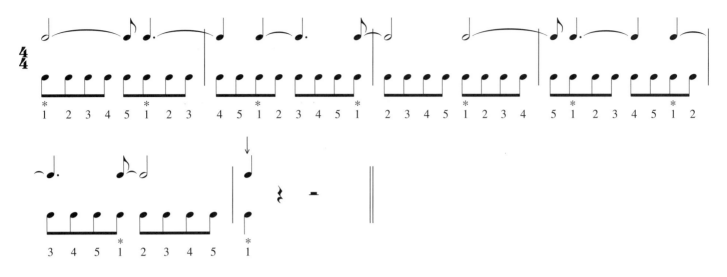

It can be helpful to calculate how many repetitions of an implied meter are needed before the pattern ends up again on beat 1. For example, it takes three measures of 4/4 for a superimposed 3/4 pattern to end up again on beat 1.

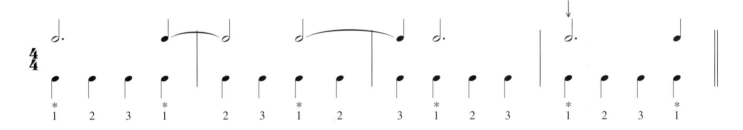

It takes five measures of 4/4 for a superimposed 5/4 pattern to end up again on beat 1.

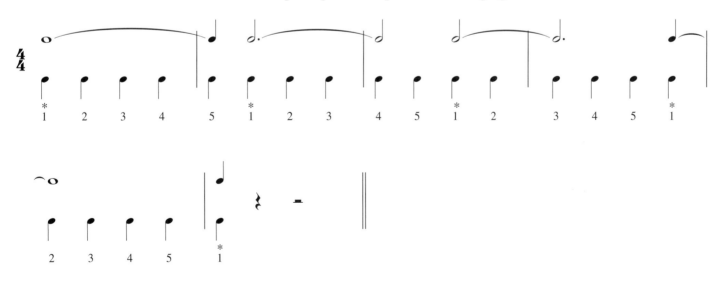

Keep in mind that you don't have to—and probably shouldn't—always start or end your patterns just on beat 1. When you superimpose a different meter, the patterns will occur at least once on every possible starting beat (if you play through its complete cycle). Just use you ears and start and end phrases in places that make musical sense.

Use this play-along track to practice tracks 78 and 79. Also practice coming up with your own variations using this rhythmic framework.

ARPEGGIO SUPERIMPOSITION

A common technique used by many of the great blues fusion masters is to superimpose an arpeggio over a different chord. The result is an extended sound created by the sum of the arpeggio against the underlying harmony. Let's take a look at why this works and explore some common substitutions.

If we extend an Amaj7 chord all the way up to the 9th, we get this:

A	C♯	E	G♯	B
1	3	5	7	9

Notice that, from the 3rd to the 9th, the notes C♯–E–G♯–B are also the same notes as a C♯m7 arpeggio. Therefore, by playing just the C♯m7 arpeggio over Amaj7, we get an Amaj9 sound without having to play a major ninth arpeggio.

To easily access and transpose these arpeggio superimpositions, it's best to think of them in terms of the starting note and the arpeggio type. For example, the superimposition we just looked at, C#m7 against Amaj7, can also be described as playing a m7 arpeggio starting on the 3rd of the maj7 chord.

There are endless possibilities with this approach (superimposing pentatonic scales, etc.), and there are *many* more combinations that are beyond the scope of this book. Here are some common superimpositions that many blues fusion artists use. You'll find some that you like better than others. Once you find the combination that you like, break it down theoretically to see what chord tones or extensions or alterations that superimposition yields. Then memorize the formula and practice transposing it to all 12 keys. To go a step beyond, one way of finding some possibilities is to use a backing track and try out every possible arpeggio you can think of against a static chord.

You'll notice that the musical examples that accompany the formulas consist of more than just running "up and down" the arpeggios. You can, and should, use the notes of the superimposed arpeggio in any combination or mix them up with other devices. The goal is to make music!

Major 7 Chords

Formula: Play a m7 arpeggio starting on the 3rd. This gives you 3–5–7–9.

This example uses a sequence based on a C#m7 arpeggio. The line starts with an eighth-note rhythm but accelerates into 16ths by beat 3 of measure 1 to create momentum.

🔊 Track 80

♩ = 120

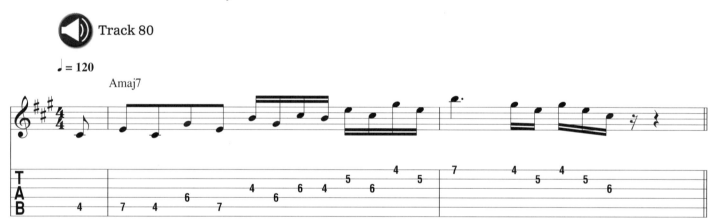

Formula: Play a maj7 arpeggio starting on the 5th. This gives you 5–7–9–#11.

As mentioned before, you don't have to just blaze through an arpeggio. You can use it as the catalyst for a musical phrase. This passage, based on superimposing the notes of an Emaj7 arpeggio over Amaj7, starts with a dotted quarter note rhythm to create a three-against-four feel. In measure 4, a bend from the 2nd (F#) to the 3rd (G#) rounds out the melody.

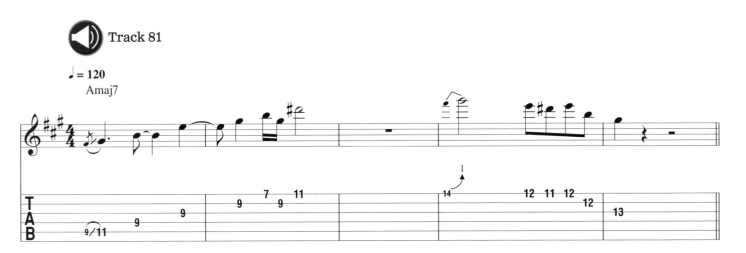

Minor 7 Chords

Formula: Play a maj7 arpeggio starting on the ♭3rd. This gives you ♭3–5–♭7–9.

This phrase uses a Cmaj7 arpeggio over Am7 to create the sound of Am9, which is further emphasized by the held B (9th) in measure 2.

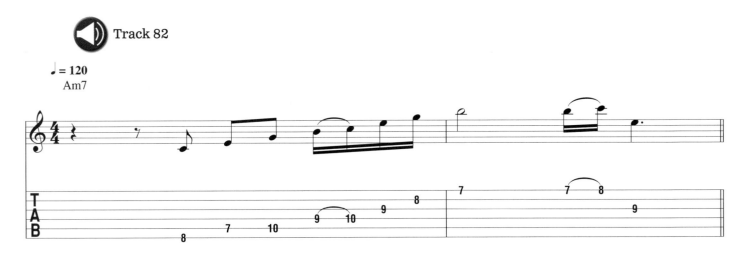

Formula: Play a m7 arpeggio starting on the 5th. This gives you the 5–♭7–9–11.

The notes of an Em7 arpeggio are used to create a melodic sequence in measures 1–2. In measure 3, the 16th/dotted eighth rhythm is broken, and the line uses faster rhythms to bring the phrase to a conclusion.

Track 83

Formula: Play a maj7 arpeggio starting on the ♭7th. This gives you the ♭7–9–11–13.

A Gmaj7 arpeggio shape is repeated over Am7 to create the sound of Am13. The phrase resolves to the 13th (F♯) of Am7, which is then bent to the ♭7th (G).

Track 84

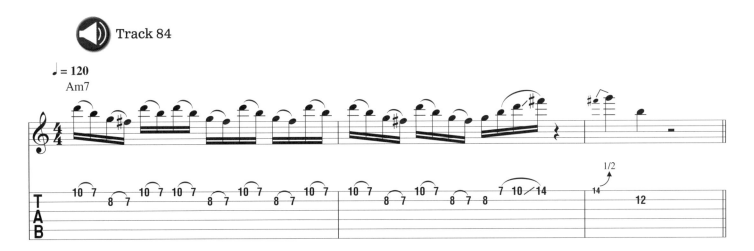

Dominant 7 Chords

Formula: Play a m7♭5 arpeggio starting on the 3rd. This gives you 3–5–♭7–9.

After a bluesy melodic phrase in measures 1–2, a C♯m7♭5 arpeggio is used as the basis for the lick that follows. Note how the arpeggio shape is broken up and zigzags up and down to create a distinguishable contour.

Track 85

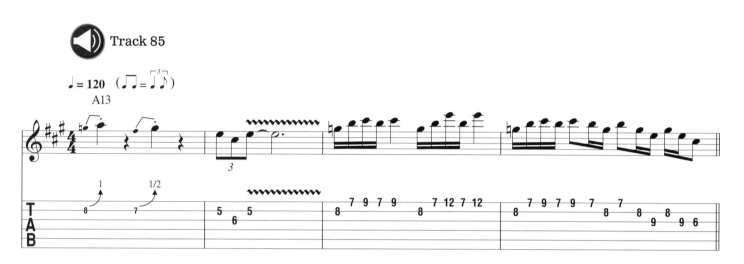

Dominant 7sus4 Chords

Formula: Play a maj7 arpeggio starting on the ♭7th. This gives you ♭7–9–11–13.

The notes of a Gmaj7 arpeggio are played in a slower descending sequence against A7sus4 in this example. Note the open sound created by this superimposition.

Track 86

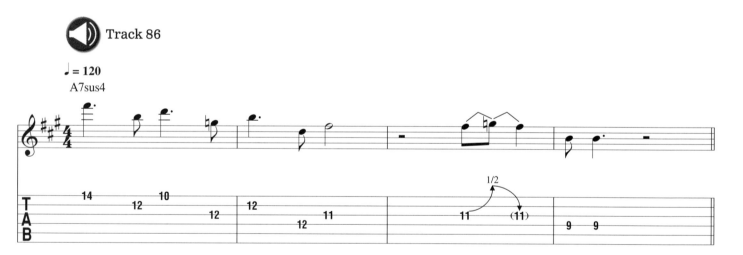

Formula: Play a m7 arpeggio starting on the 5th. This gives you 5–♭7–9–11.

Arpeggios played rapidly can generate excitement. In this example, an Em7 arpeggio is played in 16ths over A7sus4 in a high register. This is something you might hear someone like Eric Johnson do when he wants to go from a low register to a higher one really quickly. To articulate the notes played on beat 1 after the hammer-on, you can try alternate or sweep picking.

Track 87

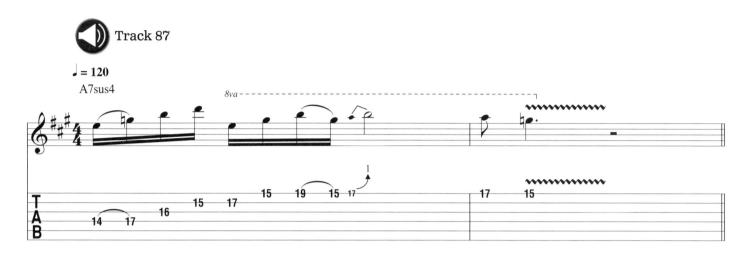

Dominant 13♯11 Chords

Formula: Play a m(maj7) arpeggio starting on the 5th. This gives you 5–♭7–9–♯11.

Multi-octave arpeggios are always exciting to hear when played fast. This lick uses a descending Em(maj7) arpeggio against A13♯11. The briefly held ♯11th (D♯) creates a momentary tension that is quickly resolved in the next beat.

Track 88

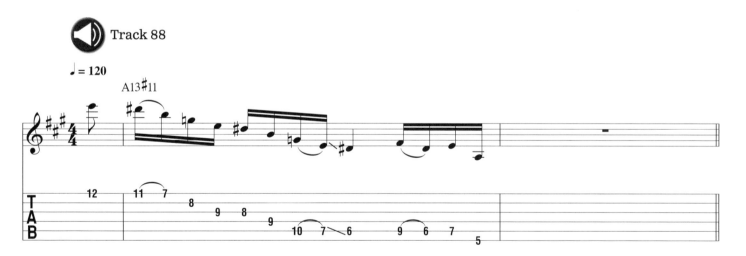

Formula: Play a maj7#5 arpeggio starting on the ♭7th. This gives you ♭7–9–#11–13.

Gmaj7#5 is superimposed over A13#11 to bring out the sound of the #11th (D#). Guitarist Mike Stern and saxophonist Michael Brecker often use repeating phrases like this to build up energy. If you find the shape in measure 1 hard to pick at this tempo, try using a sweep-picking strategy (down–up–up–up) or try pulling off from the 14th to the 11th fret on the high E string. Then use a descending sweep (up–up) to catch the notes on the B and G strings.

Track 89

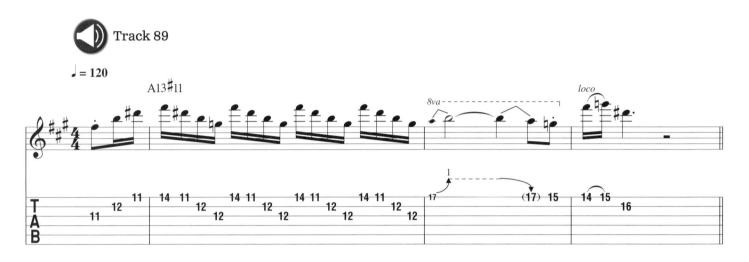

Altered Dominant Chords

Formula: Play a m(maj7) arpeggio starting on the ♭9th. This gives you ♭9–3–#5–1.

It's not necessary to start a superimposed arpeggio from the root—you can start from any degree. Here, a B♭m(maj7) arpeggio (spelled using enharmonic equivalents for ease of reading), starting from the 7th, is played over A7alt.

Track 90

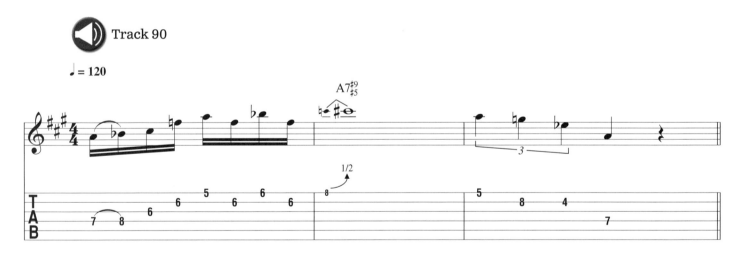

Formula: Play a m7♭5 arpeggio starting on the ♭7th. This gives you ♭7–♭9–3–♯5.

This simple phrase, based on a Gm7♭5 arpeggio played against A7alt, creates momentum via the use of a rhythmic motive (two 16ths followed by an eighth). A catchy two-note figure from the 3rd of A7 (here spelled enharmonically as D♭) to the ♭9th follows, and is repeated again down two octaves.

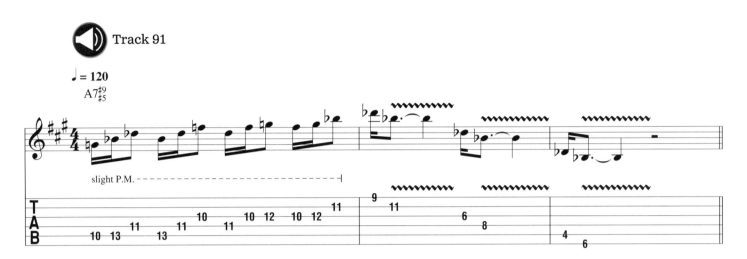

Formula: For 13♭9 chords, play major triads starting on the root, ♭3rd, ♭5th, or ♭7th. Starting on the root gives you 1–3–5, starting on the ♭3rd gives you ♭3–5–♭7, starting on the ♭5th gives you ♭5–♭7–♭9, and starting on the ♭♭7 (13) gives you ♭♭7(13)–♭9–3.

Four triads, a minor 3rd apart from each other (A, E♭, C, and F♯), and their inversions are juggled around to create some tasty dissonances over A13♭9. Try to make up your own lines using this concept. If this seems complicated, first try using only two triads—like A and E♭. Then add the others in as you gain more command.

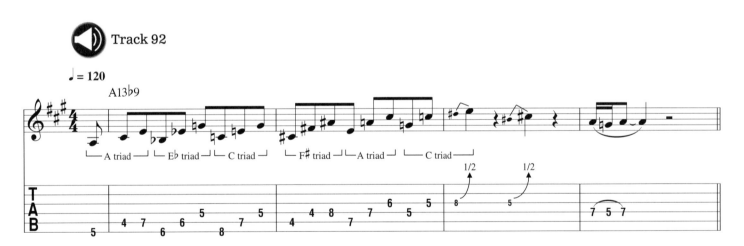

PLAYING OVER ONE-CHORD VAMPS

We've looked at some ways to play over chord changes, and some can seem a bit complicated. However, sometimes it can actually be more challenging to play over one-chord vamps, because there isn't much harmonic information to guide you.

A good way of creating activity within your lines in this regard is to use chromaticism. If resolved properly by step, any note from the chromatic scale—even the most seemingly unrelated—can be played over any chord. A very simplified way of thinking about it is that you're never more than a step away from a "right" note.

This line uses chromatic passing tones, mixed with slides and legato phrasing, to create a "smooth" line over Am7.

Track 93

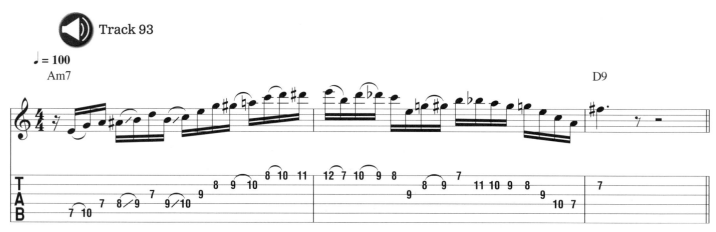

Earlier, we learned that chromatics can be used functionally—where notes that are not in key resolve by step into a chord tone—and still not sound dissonant. In some cases, players prefer *not* to resolve dissonances immediately. This creates an "outside" sound.

Sometimes players will take a shape and just move it around chromatically. This approach can work well as long as you ultimately resolve the line. In this phrase, a melodic fragment moves down chromatically before going back into an A minor tonality.

Track 94

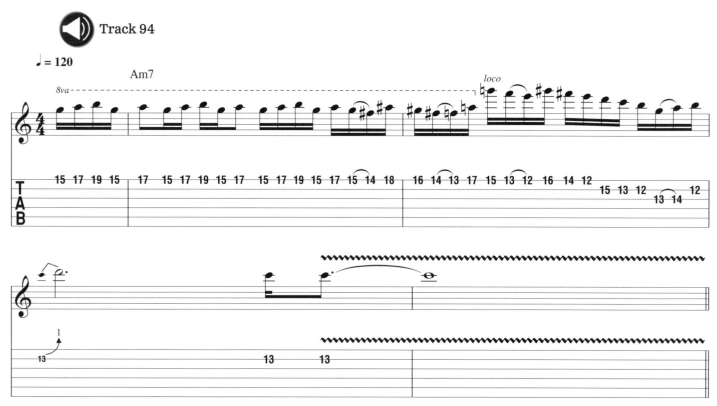

Resolution is key! This next phrase temporarily goes out of key from measure 2, beat 3 to measure 3, beat 1. Without the resolution back to the A minor tonality, this phrase might sound a little bit random.

Track 95

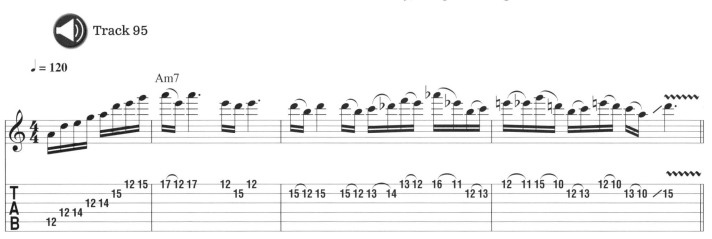

This phrase shifts out of A minor and into B♭ minor for a good amount of time. The clear resolution and the faster rhythms clearly delineate the change back into key.

Track 96

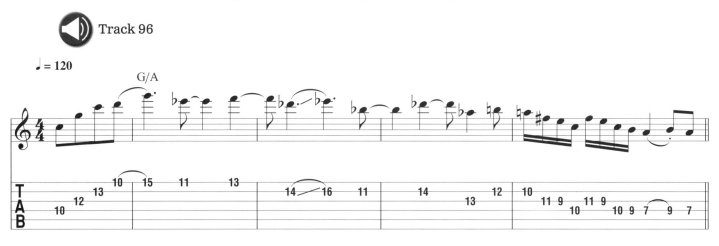

STYLISTIC LICKS

Let's close out by looking at some blues fusion phrases inspired by the masters of the genre.

Matt Schofield

The use of the 9th (G) in combination with the F blues scale gives this line a jazzy flavor without straying too far from just a pure blues sound.

Track 97

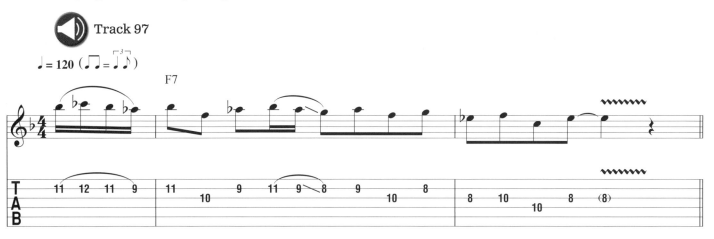

After a bend to the ♭7th of F7, a classic Charlie Parker-inspired bebop lick is played. The highlight of the phrase is the targeting of A—the 3rd of F7—on the downbeat of measure 2, with surround tones starting from measure 1, beat 3 1/2.

Track 98

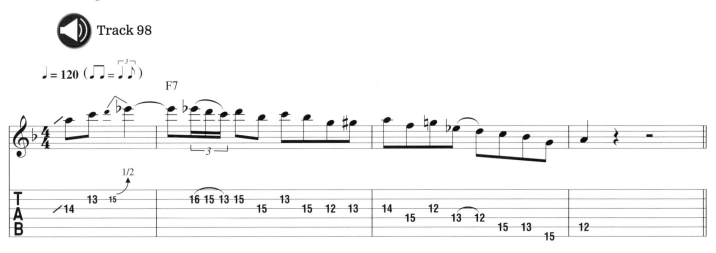

Larry Carlton

It's always nice to be able to slip in harmonically sophisticated material in a pop-type context. Here, in measure 2, the B♭ Lydian Dominant scale is used to add a splash of color.

Track 99

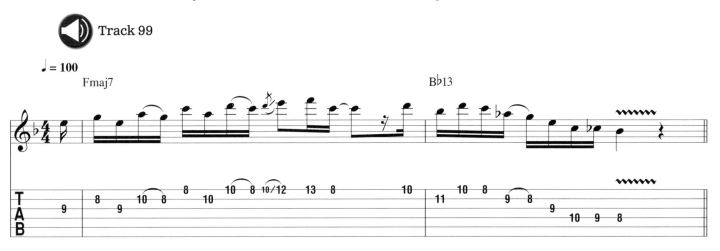

This phrase works off of arpeggiated chord shapes and uses slides and legato articulation to create a smooth sound.

Track 100

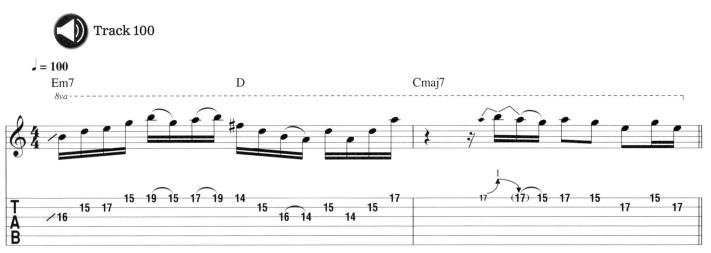

Joe Bonamassa

One thing that you'll immediately notice about Joe Bonamassa is that he's seriously fast. He often likes to run through lightning-quick pentatonic shapes like this.

Track 101

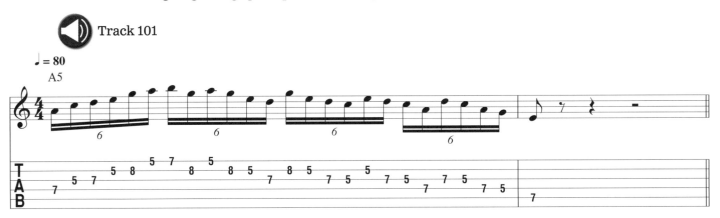

Here's another Bonamassa-inspired lick that is easy to visualize and understand but not so easy to play!

Track 102

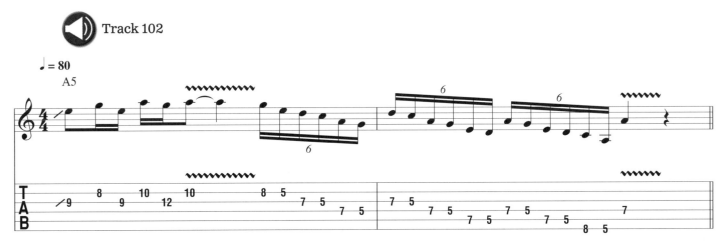

Eric Johnson

One of Eric Johnson's signature moves is to play open-voiced triad shapes up and down the neck using string skipping. This lick employs C and D open-voiced triads and inversion shapes in measure 1. By beat 3 of measure 2, coinciding with the harmonic shift, a B open-voiced triad and its inversion are introduced.

You can either alternate pick this lick or use a hybrid pick-and-fingers approach.

Track 103

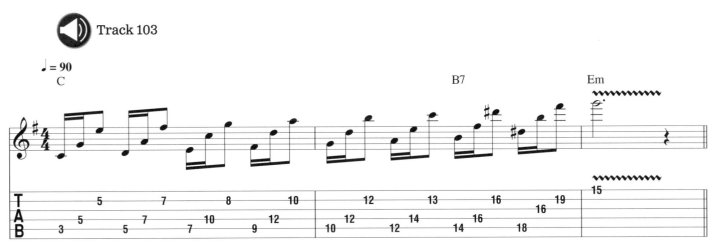

Eric Johnson also loves to play speedy arpeggiated figures that climb quickly from the low E string all to way up to the high E in the blink of an eye. This lick is based primarily on an Em7 arpeggio, played up several octaves.

Robben Ford

Robben Ford often uses the Super Locrian scale to come up with some hip lines. Over A7alt, this line here is based on A Super Locrian. Note the contours in the phrase (the lick isn't just going up and down the scale) and the melodic resolution to a simple D minor phrase in measure 2.

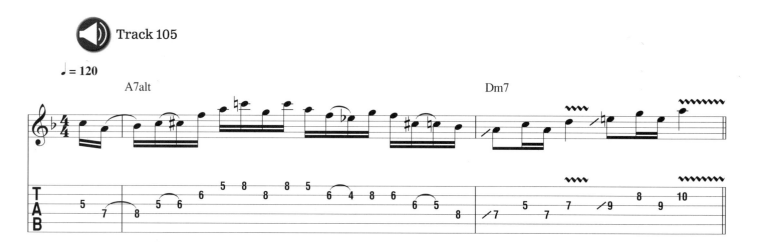

This lick mixes various D-based scales, like blues and Mixolydian, to create a slippery but distinctly bluesy sound.

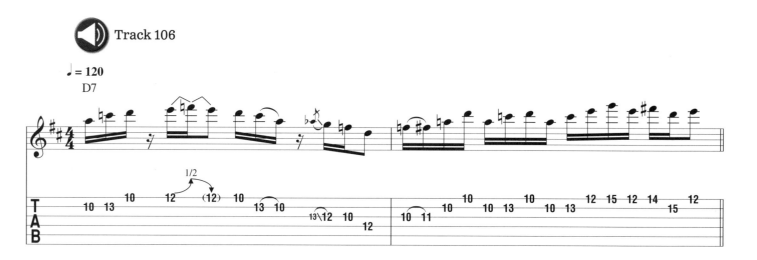

Mike Stern

Mike Stern is known for his ability to play long streams of endless lines. This lick is based primarily on D Mixolydian, but passing tones and surround tones are used to create momentum.

Track 107

B♭ Dorian is the basis for this lick, but on measure 2, beat 3, the V chord (F7) is implied with F Super Locrian to create tension, which is quickly and neatly resolved.

Track 108

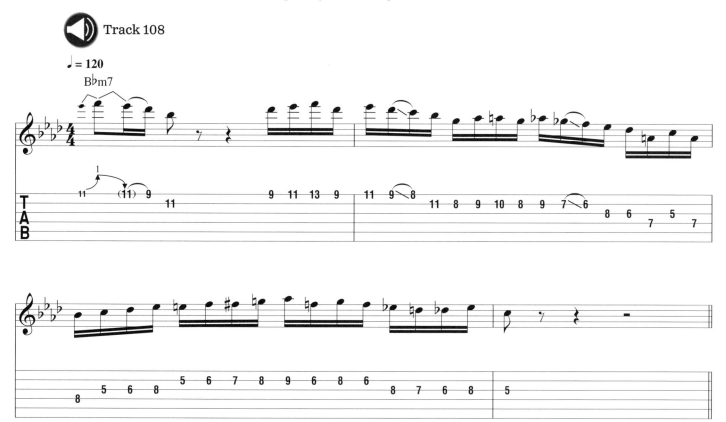

Scott Henderson

After a fiery repeating lick, all hell breaks loose in the chromatically inflected lick in measure 2. This is a good (but hard) lick to learn if you want to get some slick, chromatic ideas under your belt.

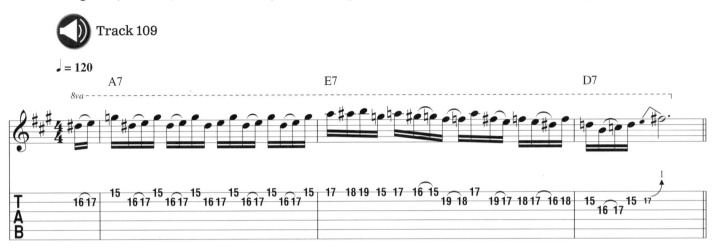

A diminished-type flavor can be created by carefully selecting certain notes to emphasize from the blues scale. The notes in the first two beats of this phrase are essentially the notes of an A diminished triad (A–C–Eb). It's the mixing of this sonority plus the pentatonic elements of the scale that give this line a unique sound.

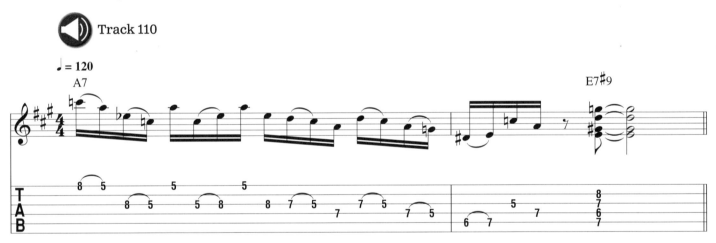

John Scofield

John Scofield is the master of creating head-scratching slippery licks. This phrase starts off with some conventional Bb7 ideas but then really goes out in the middle before resolving at the end. There are many ways to analyze this phrase. One way of looking at it is that, from measure 1, beat 4 to measure 2, beat 2, the line temporarily shifts a half step and then resolves back to the original tonality.

Track 111

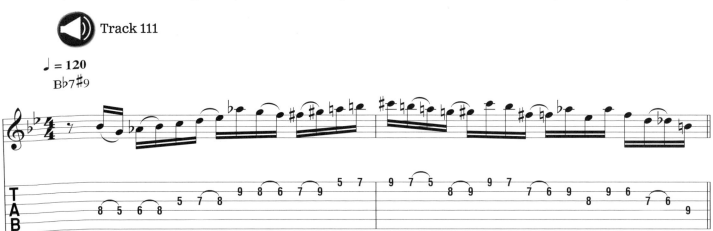

String skips and major 7th leaps are a hallmark of Scofield's style. This phrase is based mostly on E Super Locrian, and the wide interval jumps that start the line create an angular vibe.

Track 112

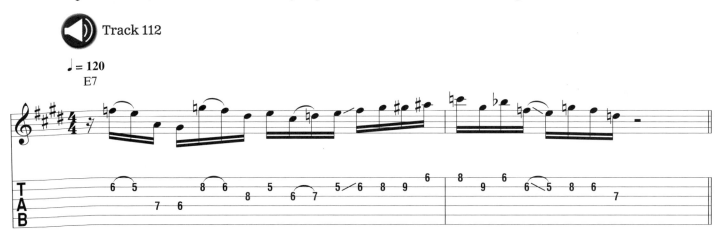

Get Better at Guitar

...with these Great Guitar Instruction Books from Hal Leonard!

101 GUITAR TIPS
INCLUDES TAB

STUFF ALL THE PROS KNOW AND USE

by Adam St. James

This book contains invaluable guidance on everything from scales and music theory to truss rod adjustments, proper recording studio set-ups, and much more. The book also features snippets of advice from some of the most celebrated guitarists and producers in the music business, including B.B. King, Steve Vai, Joe Satriani, Warren Haynes, Laurence Juber, Pete Anderson, Tom Dowd and others, culled from the author's hundreds of interviews.

00695737 Book/CD Pack..........................$16.95

AMAZING PHRASING
INCLUDES TAB

50 WAYS TO IMPROVE YOUR IMPROVISATIONAL SKILLS

by Tom Kolb

This book/CD pack explores all the main components necessary for crafting well-balanced rhythmic and melodic phrases. It also explains how these phrases are put together to form cohesive solos. Many styles are covered – rock, blues, jazz, fusion, country, Latin, funk and more – and all of the concepts are backed up with musical examples. The companion CD contains 89 demos for listening, and most tracks feature full-band backing.

00695583 Book/CD Pack..........................$19.95

BLUES YOU CAN USE
INCLUDES TAB

by John Ganapes

A comprehensive source designed to help guitarists develop both lead and rhythm playing. Covers: Texas, Delta, R&B, early rock and roll, gospel, blues/rock and more. Includes: 21 complete solos • chord progressions and riffs • turnarounds • moveable scales and more. CD features leads and full band backing.

00695007 Book/CD Pack..........................$19.95

FRETBOARD MASTERY
INCLUDES TAB

by Troy Stetina

Untangle the mysterious regions of the guitar fretboard and unlock your potential. *Fretboard Mastery* familiarizes you with all the shapes you need to know by applying them in real musical examples, thereby reinforcing and reaffirming your newfound knowledge. The result is a much higher level of comprehension and retention.

00695331 Book/CD Pack..........................$19.95

FRETBOARD ROADMAPS – 2ND EDITION

ESSENTIAL GUITAR PATTERNS THAT ALL THE PROS KNOW AND USE

by Fred Sokolow

The updated edition of this bestseller features more songs, updated lessons, and a full audio CD! Learn to play lead and rhythm anywhere on the fretboard, in any key; play a variety of lead guitar styles; play chords and progressions anywhere on the fretboard; expand your chord vocabulary; and learn to think musically – the way the pros do.

00695941 Book/CD Pack..........................$14.95

GUITAR AEROBICS
INCLUDES TAB

A 52-WEEK, ONE-LICK-PER-DAY WORKOUT PROGRAM FOR DEVELOPING, IMPROVING & MAINTAINING GUITAR TECHNIQUE

by Troy Nelson

From the former editor of *Guitar One* magazine, here is a daily dose of vitamins to keep your chops fine tuned! Musical styles include rock, blues, jazz, metal, country, and funk. Techniques taught include alternate picking, arpeggios, sweep picking, string skipping, legato, string bending, and rhythm guitar. These exercises will increase speed, and improve dexterity and pick- and fret-hand accuracy. The accompanying CD includes all 365 workout licks plus play-along grooves in every style at eight different metronome settings.

00695946 Book/CD Pack..........................$19.99

GUITAR CLUES
INCLUDES TAB

OPERATION PENTATONIC

by Greg Koch

Join renowned guitar master Greg Koch as he clues you in to a wide variety of fun and valuable pentatonic scale applications. Whether you're new to improvising or have been doing it for a while, this book/CD pack will provide loads of delicious licks and tricks that you can use right away, from volume swells and chicken pickin' to intervallic and chordal ideas. The CD includes 65 demo and play-along tracks.

00695827 Book/CD Pack..........................$19.95

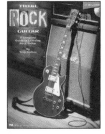

INTRODUCTION TO GUITAR TONE & EFFECTS

by David M. Brewster

This book/CD pack teaches the basics of guitar tones and effects, with audio examples on CD. Readers will learn about: overdrive, distortion and fuzz • using equalizers • modulation effects • reverb and delay • multi-effect processors • and more.

00695766 Book/CD Pack..........................$14.99

PICTURE CHORD ENCYCLOPEDIA

This comprehensive guitar chord resource for all playing styles and levels features five voicings of 44 chord qualities for all twelve keys – 2,640 chords in all! For each, there is a clearly illustrated chord frame, as well as *an actual photo* of the chord being played! Includes info on basic fingering principles, open chords and barre chords, partial chords and broken-set forms, and more.

00695224..........................$19.95

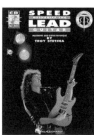

SCALE CHORD RELATIONSHIPS
INCLUDES TAB

by Michael Mueller & Jeff Schroedl

This book teaches players how to determine which scales to play with which chords, so guitarists will never have to fear chord changes again! This book/CD pack explains how to: recognize keys • analyze chord progressions • use the modes • play over nondiatonic harmony • use harmonic and melodic minor scales • use symmetrical scales such as chromatic, whole-tone and diminished scales • incorporate exotic scales such as Hungarian major and Gypsy minor • and much more!

00695563 Book/CD Pack..........................$14.95

SPEED MECHANICS FOR LEAD GUITAR
INCLUDES TAB

Take your playing to the stratosphere with the most advanced lead book by this proven heavy metal author. *Speed Mechanics* is the ultimate technique book for developing the kind of speed and precision in today's explosive playing styles. Learn the fastest ways to achieve speed and control, secrets to make your practice time really count, and how to open your ears and make your musical ideas more solid and tangible. Packed with over 200 vicious exercises including Troy's scorching version of "Flight of the Bumblebee." Music and examples demonstrated on CD. 89-minute audio.

00699323 Book/CD Pack..........................$19.95

TOTAL ROCK GUITAR
INCLUDES TAB

A COMPLETE GUIDE TO LEARNING ROCK GUITAR

by Troy Stetina

This unique and comprehensive source for learning rock guitar is designed to develop both lead and rhythm playing. It covers: getting a tone that rocks • open chords, power chords and barre chords • riffs, scales and licks • string bending, strumming, palm muting, harmonics and alternate picking • all rock styles • and much more. The examples are in standard notation with chord grids and tab, and the CD includes full-band backing for all 22 songs.

00695246 Book/CD Pack..........................$19.99